Student Study Guide

to accompany

Hole's Essentials of Human Anatomy and Physiology

Ninth Edition

David Shier

Jackie Butler

Ricki Lewis

Nancy A. Sickles Corbett, Ed. D., NP-C, RN.

Faculty, West Jersey- Memorial Family Practice Residency at Virtua
Family Nurse Practitioner, Family Medicine Center at Lumberton
Mt. Holly, NJ

Boston   Burr Ridge, IL   Dubuque, IA   Madison, WI   New York   San Francisco   St. Louis
Bangkok   Bogotá   Caracas   Kuala Lumpur   Lisbon   London   Madrid   Mexico City
Milan   Montreal   New Delhi   Santiago   Seoul   Singapore   Sydney   Taipei   Toronto

The McGraw·Hill Companies

Student Study Guide to accompany
HOLE'S ESSENTIALS OF HUMAN ANATOMY AND PHYSIOLOGY, NINTH EDITION
DAVID SHIER, JACKIE BUTLER, AND RICKI LEWIS

Published by McGraw-Hill Higher Education, an imprint of The McGraw-Hill Companies, Inc.,
1221 Avenue of the Americas, New York, NY 10020. Copyright © 2006, 2003, 2000, 1998 by
The McGraw-Hill Companies, Inc. All rights reserved.

RECYCLED

This book is printed on recycled, acid-free paper containing
10% postconsumer waste.

5 6 7 8 9 0 QPD/QPD 0 9 8 7 6

ISBN: 978-0-07-285288-2
MHID: 0-07-285288-7

www.mhhe.com

CONTENTS

TO THE STUDENT

A study guide attempts to do what the name implies: guide your study so that your learning efforts are more efficient. This study guide is based on several beliefs: (1) learning occurs best when the learner is active rather than passive;
(2) learning is easiest when the material is organized in simple units; and (3) the learner can best evaluate what he or she knows well, is unsure of, and does not know.

The study guide chapters correspond to the chapters in *Hole's Essentials of Human Anatomy and Physiology*, 9th Edition by David Shier, Jackie Butler, and Ricki Lewis. The elements of the study guide chapters and their purposes are described below.

1. *Overview.* The learning objectives at the beginning of each chapter in the text are arranged in groups according to broad, general concepts presented in the chapter. The overview also contains a purpose statement that offers a rationale for studying the chapter.

2. *Chapter Objectives.* The chapter objectives from the text are listed to help guide your study of the chapter.

3. *Focus Question.* The focus question helps you focus your study of each chapter.

4. *Mastery Test.* The mastery test, taken before reading the chapter, is designed to help you identify:

    a.   concepts you already know,

    b.   concepts you need to clarify, and

    c.   concepts you do not know.

    If you are using a study guide for the first time, you may be unfamiliar with this type of testing. It is important for you to realize that this test is *for your information.* Its purpose is to help you learn where to concentrate your learning efforts; therefore, it is best not to guess at any answers.

5. *Study Activities.* A variety of study activities help facilitate the study of the principal ideas of each chapter.

The study activities should be done after you have read the chapter carefully, concentrating on those areas that the mastery test indicates you do not know.

The first activity in each unit is a vocabulary exercise, concentrating on word parts appropriate to each chapter. You are asked to define these as you understand them and then compare your definitions with those in the chapter. You may find it helpful to define terms orally and in writing. If you have a tape recorder, you may wish to use it as a study device.

After the vocabulary exercise, you may be asked to describe a process, label a diagram, fill in a chart, or observe the function of a body part in yourself or in a partner. (This partner may be a classmate or a family member.) These are written activities, but you may also find it helpful to repeat them orally.

After you complete the study activities, retake the mastery test. A comparison of the two scores will indicate the progress you have made. You may also wish to set a learning goal for yourself, such as a score of 70 percent, 80 percent, or 90 percent on the mastery test after completing your study of a chapter. If you have not attained your goal, the mastery test results can show where you need additional study.

The answers to the mastery test are at the end of the study guide. You can compare your responses to the review activities by referring to the appropriate page numbers in the text. Each major section in the study guide is identified by a Roman numeral and the title of the corresponding section in the text. The activities in the study guide are lettered, and the corresponding pages in the text are noted after the activity.

You are responsible for your own learning; no teacher can assume that responsibility. A study guide can help you direct your study more efficiently, but only you can control how well and how completely you use the guide.

UNIT I
LEVELS OF ORGANIZATION

CHAPTER 1
INTRODUCTION TO HUMAN ANATOMY AND PHYSIOLOGY

OVERVIEW

This chapter begins the study of anatomy and physiology by defining the disciplines (objective 1) and by explaining the characteristics and needs that are common to all living things (objectives 2 and 3). It introduces a basic mechanism necessary to maintain life (objective 4), as well as the relationship of increasingly complex levels of organization in humans (objective 5). The study of levels of organization continues with the identification of body cavities and the organs to be found within each cavity (objective 6). Finally, the language used to describe relative positions of body parts, body sections, and body regions is presented (objective 7).

This chapter defines the characteristics and needs common to all living things, and the manner in which the human body is organized to accomplish life processes. The language peculiar to anatomy and physiology is also introduced.

CHAPTER OBJECTIVES

After you have studied this chapter, you should be able to:

1.1   Introduction
       1. Describe the early studies into the workings of the human body.

1.2   Anatomy and Physiology
       2. Define *anatomy* and *physiology,* and explain how they are related.

1.3   Characteristics of Life
       3. List and describe the major characteristics of life.

1.4   Maintenance of Life
       4. List and describe the major requirements of organisms.
       5. Define *homeostasis,* and explain its importance to survival.
       6. Describe a homeostatic mechanism.

1.5   Levels of Organization
       7. Explain biological levels of organization.

1.6   Organization of the Human Body
       8. Describe the locations of the major body cavities.
       9. List the organs located in each major body cavity.
     10. Name the membranes associated with the thoracic and abdominopelvic cavities.
     11. Name the major organ systems and list the organs associated with each.
     12. Describe the general functions of each organ system.

1.7   Anatomical Terminology
     13. Properly use the terms that describe relative positions, body sections, and body regions.

FOCUS QUESTION

How does knowledge of anatomy and physiology facilitate communication about body structure and function between scientists and health care professionals?

MASTERY TEST

Now take the mastery test. Do not guess. As soon as you complete the test, correct it. Note your successes and failures so that you can read the chapter to meet your learning needs.

1. Study of the human body first began with earliest humans because
   a. our early ancestors were curious about the world around them.
   b. they were as interested in their body parts and their functions as we are today.
   c. of their concern with illness and injury.

2. Which of the following factors sets the stage for early knowledge of the human body?
   a. a belief that spirits or gods controlled sickness and health
   b. the growing experience of medicine men as they treated the sick with herbs and potions
   c. the belief that natural processes were caused by forces that could be understood
   d. the ability to ask questions and record the answers

3. The development of modern science began with:
   a. rejection of the belief in supernatural forces
   b. the growing experience of medicine men in the treatment of illness and injury
   c. the belief that natural processes were caused by forces that could be understood
   d. the ability to ask questions and record the answers

4. What languages form the basis of the language of anatomy and physiology?

5. The branch of science that deals with the structure of body parts is _____ .

6. The branch of science that studies how body parts function is_____ .

7. The function of a part is (always, sometimes, never) related to its structure.

8. While knowledge of physiology continues to develop, knowledge of anatomy does not change.
   a. True
   b. False

9. List those characteristics that humans share with other organisms.
   a.   f.
   b.   g.
   c.   h.
   d.   i.
   e.   j.

10. Does statement *a* explain statement *b*?
    a. Vital signs are a result of metabolic activities.
    b. Death is recognized by the absence of vital signs.

11. The most abundant chemical in the human body is _____ .

12. Food is used as a(n) _____ source to build new _____ _____ , and to participate in the regulation of chemical reactions.

13. Oxygen is used to release _____ .

14. An increase in temperature _____ the rate of chemical reactions.

15. The action of the heart creates _____ pressure in the blood vessels.

16. Homeostasis means
    a. maintenance of a stable internal environment.
    b. integrating the functions of the various organ systems.
    c. preventing any change in the organism.

17. Match the terms related to homeostasis in column A to the definitions in column B.

a. homeostasis

b. receptors

c. effectors

d. set point

1. ____ a point which tells what a particular value should be

2. ____ provide information about specific conditions in the internal environment

3. ____ cause responses which alter conditions in the internal environment

18. List the levels of organization of the body in order of increasing complexity, beginning with the cell.

_____

19. The portion of the body that contains the head, neck, and trunk is called the _____.

20. The arms and legs are called the _____ portion.

21. The two major cavities of the axial portion of the body are the _____ cavity and the _____ cavity.

22. The inferior boundary of the thoracic cavity is the _____.

23. The heart, esophagus, trachea, and thymus gland are located in the _____, which separates the thoracic cavity into two compartments.

24. The pelvic cavity is

a.   the portion of the abdominopelvic cavity below the pelvic brim.

b.   the portion of the abdomen that contains the internal reproductive organs and the urinary bladder.

c.   the portion of the abdomen surrounded by the bones of the pelvis.

25. List the four body cavities located in the head.

26. The visceral and parietal pleural membranes secrete a serous fluid into a potential space called the

_____ _____.

27. The heart is covered by the_____ membranes.

28. The peritoneal membranes are located in the _____ cavity.

29. The covering of the body is made of an organ and various accessory organs known as the_____ system.

30. Match the systems listed in the first column with the functions listed in the second column.

_____ a. nervous system

_____ b. muscular system

_____ c. circulatory system

_____ d. respiratory system

_____ e. skeletal system

_____ f. digestive system

_____ g. lymphatic system

_____ h. endocrine system

_____ i. urinary system

_____ j. reproductive system

1. reproduction

2. processing and transporting

3. integration and coordination

4. support and movement

31. Which of the following positions of body parts is(are) in *anatomic* position?

a.   palms of hands turned toward sides of body

b.   standing erect

c.   arms at side

d.   face toward left shoulder

32. Terms of relative position are used to describe the

a.   relationship of siblings within a family.

b.   importance of the various functions of organ systems in maintaining life.

c.   location of one body part with respect to another.

33. A sagittal section divides the body into

a.   superior and inferior portions.

b.   right and left portions.

c.   anterior and posterior portions.

34. The terms *epigastric, hypochondriac,* and *iliac* are examples of _____ _____.

STUDY ACTIVITIES

I. Aids to Understanding Words

Define the following word parts. (p. 2)

append-	pariet-
cardi-	pelv-
cran-	peri-
dors-	pleur-
homeo-	-stasis
-logy	-tomy
meta-	

II. 1.1 Introduction (p. 2)

A.   How did ancient healers begin their study of the human body? (p. 2)

B.   How did the scientific study of the human body begin?

III. 1.2 Anatomy and Physiology (pp. 2–3)

A.   Explain how the structure of the fingers is related to their grasping function.

B.   Are new discoveries more likely in anatomy or physiology? Explain your answer.

IV. 1.5 Levels of Organization (pp. 3–4)

Arrange the following structures in increasing levels of complexity: atoms, organ systems, organelles, organism, organs, macromolecules, cells, tissues, molecules.

V. 1.3 Characteristics of Life (p. 4)

A. Describe the following characteristics of life. (p. 4)

movement

responsiveness

growth

reproduction

respiration

digestion

absorption

assimilation

circulation

excretion

B. What is metabolism?

VI. Maintenance of Life (pp. 5–8)

A. Match the terms in the first column with the statements in the second column that define their role in the maintenance of life.

_____ 1. water	a. essential for metabolic processes
_____ 2. food	b. governs the rate of chemical reactions
_____ 3. oxygen	c. creates a pressing or compressing action
_____ 4. heat	d. necessary for release of energy
_____ 5. pressure	e. provides chemicals for building new living matter

B. Why are observations of the vital signs important to nurses and physicians?

C.   Homeostasis (pp. 5–8)

      1.   Define *homeostasis*. Include the functions of receptors, effectors, and a set point.

      2.   How is body temperature maintained at 37°C (98.6°F)?

      3.   Describe negative and positive feedback mechanisms. Give examples of each.

VII.   1.6 Organization of the Human Body (pp. 8–14)

A.   List the components of the axial appendicular cavities.

B.   1. List the contents of the thoracic cavity.

      2. List the contents of the abdominopelvic cavity.

C.   List the four smaller cavities of the body.

D.   Thoracic and Abdominopelvic Membranes (pp. 8–11)

      1.   Fill in the blanks.
         a.   The walls of the thoracic cavity are lined with a membrane called the _____
          _____.
         b.   The lungs are covered by the _____ _____ .
         c.   Why is the pleural cavity called a potential space?

      2.   Name and describe the membranes covering the heart.

      3.   The linings of the abdominopelvic cavity are the _____ _____ and the
         _____ _____.

E.   Organ Systems

Fill in the following table. (pp. 11–14)

Structure and function of organ systems

Function	Organ system	Function
Support and Movement	1.	
	2.	
Integration and Coordination	1.	
	2.	
Transport	1.	
	2.	
	3.	
Absorption and Excretion	1.	
	2.	
	3.	
Reproduction: Female	1.	
Male	2.	

VIII.   Anatomical Terminology (pp. 14–17)

A.   Using this illustration, specify the terms that describe the relationship of one point on the body to another. (p. 14)

1.   Point (*a*) in relation to point (*d*).

2.   Point (*f*) in relation to point (*h*).

3.   Point (*g*) in relation to point (*i*).

4.   Point (*l*) in relation to point (*j*).

5.   Point (*i*) in relation to point (*g*).

6.   Point (*c*) in relation to point (*a*).

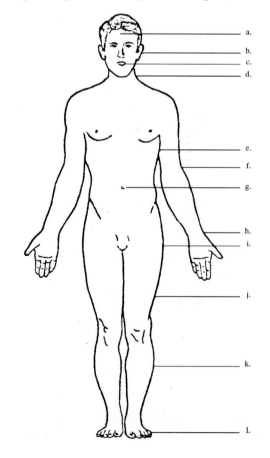

B.　　Using the illustration on the previous page, perform the following exercises. (pp. 14–17)

    1.　　Draw a line through the drawing to indicate a midsagittal section. How is this different from a frontal section?

    2.　　Draw a line through the drawing to indicate a transverse section.

    3.　　Define *cross section, longitudinal section,* and *oblique section.*

    4.　　Locate and label the following body regions on the diagram: epigastric, umbilical, hypogastric, hypochondriac, lumbar, and iliac. Locate these regions on yourself or on a partner.

    5.　　Locate and label the following body parts on the diagram: antebrachium, antecubital, axillary, brachial, buccal, cervical, groin, inguinal, mammary, ophthalmic, palmar, and pectoral.

IX.　Clinical Focus Question

List the organs and/or systems whose structure and function should be assessed to diagnose the cause of the following symptoms.

When you have finished the study activities to your satisfaction, retake the mastery test and compare your results with your initial attempt. If you are not satisfied with your performance, repeat the appropriate study activities.

OVERVIEW

This chapter introduces some basic concepts of chemistry, a science that studies the composition of substances and the changes that occur as basic elements combine. It explains how substances combine to make up matter (objectives 1–5), how substances are classified as an acid or a base (objective 6), and the organic and inorganic substances that make up the living cell (objectives 7 and 8).

Knowledge of basic chemical concepts enhances understanding of the functions of cells and of the human body.

CHAPTER OBJECTIVES

After you have studied this chapter, you should be able to:

2.1   Introduction

   1.   Explain how the study of living material depends on the study of chemistry.

2.2   Structure of Matter

   2.   Discuss how atomic structure determines how atoms interact.

   3.   Describe the relationships between atoms and molecules.

   4.   Explain how molecular and structural formulas symbolize the composition of compounds.

   5.   Describe three types of chemical reactions.

   6.   Define pH.

2.3   Chemical Constituents of Cells

   7.   List the major groups of inorganic chemicals common in cells.

   8.   Describe the functions of various types of organic chemicals in cells.

FOCUS QUESTION

How is chemistry related to the structure and function of living things and their parts?

MASTERY TEST

Now take the mastery test. Do not guess. As soon as you complete the test, correct it. Note your successes and failures so that you can read the chapter to meet your learning needs.

   1.   Excess iron and iron deficiency lead to abnormal function.

   a.   true   b.   false

   2.   The branch of science that deals with the composition of substances is _____ .

   3.   What is matter? In what forms can it be found?

   4.   The substances that comprise all matter are called _____ .

   5.   What four elements are most plentiful in the human body?

   6.   An atom is made of

   a.   a nucleus.   d.   electrons.

   b.   protons.   e.   all of the above.

   c.   neutrons.

   7.   Match the following.

   _____ a.   neutron   1.   positive electrical charge

   _____ b.   proton   2.   negative electrical charge

   _____ c.   electron   3.   no electrical charge

8. The atomic number of an element is determined by the number of _____ .

9. When atoms combine, they gain or lose
   a. electrons.
   b. neutrons.
   c. protons.
   d. nuclei.

10. Atoms that have the same atomic numbers but different atomic weights are
    a. catalysts.
    b. neutrinos.
    c. isotopes.
    d. heliotropes.

11. An element is inactive if _____ .

12. The atomic weight of an element is determined by the number of _____ _____ _____ .

13. An ion is
    a. an atom that is electrically charged.
    b. an atom that has gained an electron.
    c. an atom that has lost an electron.
    d. all of the above.

14. An ionic bond is created by
    a. a positive and a negative ion attracting each other.
    b. two or more positive ions combining.
    c. two or more negative ions combining.

15. In forming a covalent bond, electrons are
    a. shared by two atoms.
    b. given up by an atom.
    c. taken up by an atom.
    d. none of the above.

16. Water is formed by molecules of hydrogen and oxygen united by a _____ bond.

17. A compound is formed when atoms of _____ elements combine.

18. $C_6H_{12}O_6$ is an example of a(n) _____ formula.

19.

is an example of a(n) _____ formula.

20. Two major types of chemical reactions are called _____ and _____ .

21. The symbol $\rightleftharpoons$ indicates a(n) _____ reaction.

22. An atom or molecule that affects the rate of a reaction without being consumed by the reaction is called a(n) _____ .

23. An electrolyte that releases hydrogen ions in water is a(n) _____ .

24. Electrolytes that release ions that combine with hydrogen ions are called _____ .

25. The pH measures concentration of _____ _____ .

26. What is the pH of a neutral solution?

27. An inorganic substance that releases ions when it reacts with water is known as a(n) _____ .

28. Identify the following cell constituents with an O if they are organic and an I if they are inorganic.
    a. water ( )
    b. carbohydrate ( )
    c. glucose ( )
    d. oxygen ( )
    e. protein ( )
    f. fats ( )

29. Carbohydrate molecules contain atoms of _____ , _____ , and _____ .

30. Fat molecules contain _____ and _____ .

31. Fats, phospholipids, and steroids are important _____ found in the human cell.

32. An enzyme is a(n) _____ that acts as a catalyst.

33. When an egg white hardens when exposed to heat, it has been _____ .

34. The function of nucleic acids is to
   a. store information and control life processes.
   b. act as receptors for hydrogen ions.
   c. neutralize bases within the cell.

STUDY ACTIVITIES

I. Aids to Understanding Words

Define the following word parts. (pp. 30–31)

di-   mono-

glyc-   poly-

lip-   sacchar-

-lyt   syn-

II. 2.1 Introduction (p. 31)

A.   What is the subject matter of chemistry?

B.   Why is chemistry essential to understanding body structure and function?

III. 2.2 Structure of Matter (pp. 31–38)

A.   Answer these questions concerning elements and atoms. (pp. 31–32)
   1. Anything that has weight and takes up space is _____ .
   2. Basic substances are called _____ .
   3. Tiny, invisible particles that comprise basic substances are called _____ .
   4. Two or more particles of the same basic substance form a(n) _____ .
   5. The particles found in the nucleus of an atom are _____ and _____ .
   6. The particle that moves around the nucleus of an atom and carries a negative electrical charge is the _____ .

B.   Fill in the table. (p. 31)

Element	Symbol	Element	Symbol
Oxygen		Sodium	
Carbon		Magnesium	
	H	Cobalt	
Nitrogen			Cu
	Ca		F
	P	Iodine	
	K		Fe
Sulfur			Mn
	Cl	Zinc	

11

C.   Answer these questions that pertain to the accompanying illustration. (pp. 32–34)

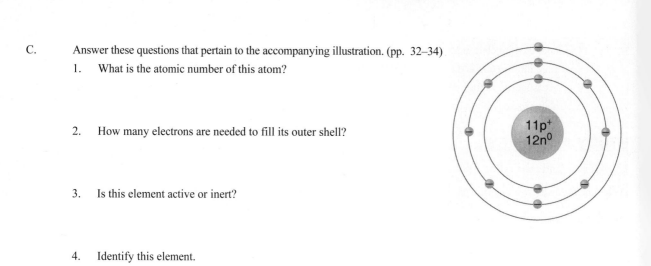

1.   What is the atomic number of this atom?

2.   How many electrons are needed to fill its outer shell?

3.   Is this element active or inert?

4.   Identify this element.

D.   1.   Draw diagrams of an ionic bond (electrovalent bond) and a covalent bond. (pp. 33–36)

2.   How are these bonds different?

3.   Describe a polar molecule and its hydrogen bond.

E.   Answer the following questions about radioactive isotopes. (p. 34)

1.   Describe the difference between a stable isotope and a radioactive isotope.

2.   Why are isotopes useful in the treatment of cancer?

F.   Answer these questions that pertain to the accompanying diagram. (pp. 36–38)

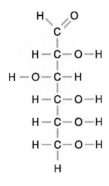

1.   Give the molecular formula of this substance.

2.   Identify this compound.

3.   Is it an organic or an inorganic substance? Why?

G.   Label the following chemical reactions. (p. 37)
    1. $A + B \rightarrow AB$ _____
    2. $AB \rightarrow A + B$ _____
    3. $A + B \rightleftharpoons AB$ _____

H.   Answer these questions concerning acid and base concentrations. (p. 38)
    1.   What is meant by pH?

    2.   Substances that release hydrogen ions (H^+) in water are called _____.
    3.   Substances that release ions that combine with hydrogen ions are _____.
    4.   Identify these substances as either acid or base.
    carrot: pH 5.0   tomato: pH 4.2
    milk of magnesia: pH 10.5   lemon: pH 2.3
    human blood: pH 7.4   distilled water: pH 7.0
    5.   What is the range of pH within which the human organism can survive?

IV.   2.3 Chemical Constituents of Cells (pp. 39–46)

A.   What roles do the following inorganic substances play in the cell? Be specific. (p. 39)
    water   carbon dioxide

    oxygen   inorganic salts (Na^+, K^+, Ca^{+2}, HCO_3^-, PO_4^{-3})

B.   Answer these questions concerning carbohydrates. (p. 39–40)
    1.   What is the role of carbohydrates in maintaining the cell?

2. The form of carbohydrate utilized by the cell is _____ .

3. Humans store carbohydrates in the form of _____ .

4. Describe monosaccharides, disaccharides, and polysaccharides.

C. Answer these questions concerning lipids. (pp. 40–42)

1. What is the role of lipids in maintaining the cell?

2. Fats are composed of _____ _____ ,
   and _____ .

3. Fats containing single carbon-carbon bonds are _____ .

4. Fats containing one or more double-bonded carbon atoms are _____ .

5. Describe the molecular structure of these lipids.
   triglycerides

   phospholipids

   steroids

6. Identify the characteristics and functions of these lipids.
   triglycerides

   phospholipids

   steroids

D. Answer these questions concerning proteins. (pp. 43–45)

1. What is the role of protein in maintaining the cell?

2. The building materials of a protein are _____ _____ .

3. The shape of protein molecules is maintained by its _____ _____ _____ .

4. A protein molecule that has become disorganized and lost its shape is said to be _____ .

E. Nucleic Acids (pp. 45–46)

1. The nucleic acids are _____ and _____ .

2. What is their role in cell function?

V.   **Clinical Focus Question**

1.   Why is it important for human beings to have an adequate amount of water?

2.   What is likely to happen to chemical activity if the body is deprived of adequate amounts of water?

3.   List mechanisms by which an individual may become deficient in water.

When you have finished the study activities to your satisfaction, retake the mastery test and compare your results with your initial attempt. If you are not satisfied with your performance, repeat the appropriate study activities.

OVERVIEW

This chapter deals with the structural unit of the human body—the cell. It explains how cells vary from each other, the makeup of a composite cell, and the contribution of each organelle to cellular function (objectives 1–4). The nucleus and its parts are described (objective 5). It introduces the various mechanisms used to transport material into and out of the cell (objective 6). The life cycle of a cell, including the processes of cell reproduction and cell death, is explained (objectives 7–10).

An understanding of cell structure is basic to understanding how cells support life at the cellular and organismic levels.

CHAPTER OBJECTIVES

After you have studied this chapter, you should be able to:

3.1   Introduction

    1.   Explain how cells differ from one another.

3.2   Composite Cell

    2.   Describe the characteristics of a composite cell.

    3.   Explain how the structure of a cell membrane makes possible its functions.

    4.   Describe each type of cytoplasmic organelle, and explain its function.

    5.   Describe the parts of the cell nucleus and its function.

3.3   Movements through Cell Membranes

    6.   Explain how substances move through cell membranes.

3.4   The Cell Cycle

    7.   Describe the cell cycle.

    8.   Explain how a cell divides.

    9.   Discuss what happens when a cell specializes.

    10.   Describe how cell death is a normal part of development.

FOCUS QUESTION

How does the structure of cellular organelles contribute to and support the functions of the organelle and, in turn, the cell?

MASTERY TEST

Now take the mastery test. Do not guess. As soon as you complete the test, correct it. Note your successes and failures so that you can read the chapter to meet your learning needs.

1.   The cells of the human body vary in terms of size and _____ .

2.   The cell form is

    a.   two dimensional.

    b.   three dimensional.

3.   Which of the following statements about a hypothetical composite cell is(are) true?

    a.   It is necessary to construct a composite cell because cells vary so much, based on their function.

    b.   It contains structures that occur in many kinds of cells.

    c.   It contains structures that occur only in all cells, although the characteristics of the structure may vary.

    d.   It is an actual cell type chosen because it occurs most commonly in the body.

4. The two major portions of the cell, each of which is surrounded by a membrane, are the
   _____ and the _____ .

5. The organelles are located in the
   a. nucleolus.   c. cell matrix.
   b. cytoplasm.   d. cell membrane.

6. The cell membrane allows some substances to pass through it and excludes others. This is possible because the cell
   membrane is _____ _____ .

7. Bacteria are simpler cells than human cells and contain
   a. only organelles.   c. neither organelles nor a nucleus.
   b. a very small nucleus.

8. The cell membrane is composed of a double layer of
   a. protein molecules.   c. polysaccharide molecules.
   b. phospholipid molecules.   d. amino acids.

9. The inner layer of the cell membrane composed of the fatty acid portion of lipid molecules is *impermeable* to
   molecules that are soluble in _____ .

10. Protein molecules embedded in the phospholipids of the cell membrane that span the cell membrane are known as
    _____ _____ or _____ _____ proteins.

11. Examples of ions that move across the cell membrane are _____ and _____ .

12. The organelle that functions as a system of transport for materials from one part of the cytoplasm to another is the
    _____ _____ .

13. Ribosomes function in the synthesis of protein molecules.
    a. true   b. false

14. The Golgi apparatus is involved in the "packaging" of proteins for secretion to the (inside, outside) of the cell.

15. The mitochondria function in the release of _____ to the cells.

16. The enzymes of the lysosome function to
    a. control cell reproduction.   c. release energy from where it is stored within the
    b. digest bacteria and damaged cell parts.   cell.
                                                     d. control the Krebs cycle.

17. Peroxisomes are abundant in the _____ and the _____ .

18. Microfilaments are rods of protein involved in cellular_____ .

19. Which of the following statements about the centrosome is(are) true?
    a. It is located near the nucleus.   c. The centrosome is concerned with the
    b. The centrioles of the centrosome function   distribution of chromosomes.
       solely in reproduction.   d. All of the above are true.

20. Cilia are found on the surface of
    a. endothelial cells.   c. epidermal cells.
    b. epithelial cells.   d. mucosa.

21. The structures that float in the nucleoplasm of the nucleus are the _____ and the
    _____ .

22. The difference between active and passive mechanisms of movement through cell membranes is that active
    mechanisms require_____ _____ .

23. The process that allows the movement of gases and ions from areas of higher concentration to areas of lower
    concentration until equilibrium has been achieved is called_____ .

24. The process by which nonsoluble material moves through the cell membrane by using a carrier molecule is called
    _____ _____ .

25. The process by which water moves across a semipermeable membrane from areas of low concentration of solute to
    areas of higher concentration is called _____ .

26. A hypertonic solution is one that
   a. contains a greater concentration of solute than the cell.
   b. contains the same concentration of solute as the cell.
   c. contains a lesser concentration of solute than the cell.

27. The process by which molecules are forced through a membrane by pressure that is greater on one side than on the other side is called _____ .

28. The process that uses energy to move ions across a concentration gradient from an area of lower concentration to an area of higher concentration is called _____ _____ .

29. The process by which cells engulf liquid molecules is called _____ .

30. A process that allows cells to take in molecules of solids is called _____ .

31. Once solid material is taken into a vacuole, which of the following statements best describes what happens?
   a. A ribosome enters the vacuole and uses the amino acids in the invader to form new protein.
   b. A lysosome combines with the vacuole and digests the enclosed solid material.
   c. The vacuole remains separated from the cytoplasm, and the solid material persists unchanged.
   d. Oxygen enters the vacuole and burns the enclosed solid material.

32. The process that ensures duplication of DNA molecules during cell reproduction is _____ .

33. Match these events with their correct descriptions.

   _____ a. prophase
   _____ b. metaphase
   _____ c. anaphase
   _____ d. telophase

   1. Microtubules shorten; chromosomes are pulled toward centrioles.
   2. Chromatin forms chromosomes; nuclear envelope and nucleolus break up and disperse.
   3. Chromosomes elongate; nuclear membranes form around each chromosome set.
   4. Chromosomes become arranged midway between centrioles; duplicate parts of chromosomes become separated.

34. The process by which cells develop unique characteristics in structure and function is called_____ .

STUDY ACTIVITIES

I. Aids to Understanding Words

Define the following word parts. (p. 50)

cyt-   iso-

endo-   mit-

hyper-   phag-

hypo-   pino-

inter-   -som

II. Introduction (p. 50)

The unit of life of human beings is the _____ .

Explain your response.

III. 3.2 Composite Cell (pp. 50–59)

A.   Answer the following questions about the cell membrane. (pp. 52–54)

1.   Chemically, the cell membrane is mainly composed of _____, _____ and _____.

2.   Describe the role of lipid molecules in making the cell membrane semipermeable.

3.   Where are carbohydrate molecules located?

4.   What is their function?

B.   Fill in the following table: (pp. 54–59)

Structure and function of cellular organelles

Organelles	Structure	Function
Cell membrane		
Endoplasmic reticulum		
Ribosomes		
Golgi apparatus		
Mitochondria		
Lysosomes		
Peroxisomes		
Microfilaments and microtubules		
Centrosome		
Cilia and flagella		
Vesicles		
Nuclear envelope		
Nucleolus		
Chromatin		

IV.   3.3 Movements through Cell Membranes (pp. 59–65)

A.   Answer these questions concerning movement through cell membranes. (pp. 59–62)

1.   In what direction do the molecules of solute move in diffusion?

2.   When does diffusion stop?

3. What substances in the human body are transported by diffusion?

4. What is dialysis? Describe how it is used in an artificial kidney.

5. Describe facilitated diffusion.

6. How does osmosis differ from diffusion?

B. Below are three drawings of a red blood cell in solutions of varying tonicity. Label the tonicity of the solution in each drawing, and explain what is happening and why. (p. 62)

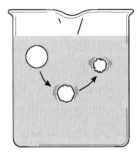 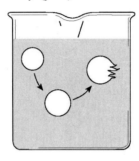 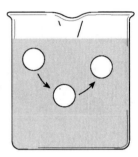

C. Answer these questions concerning the accompanying illustration. (p. 63)

1. What process is illustrated here?

2. What provides the force needed to pull the liquid through the solids?

3. Where does this process occur within the body?

Filter paper

Water and solids

Gravitational force

Solids

Water

D.   Answer the questions concerning the accompanying diagram. (p. 63)

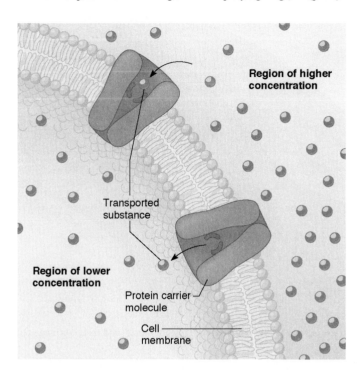

1.   What transport mechanism is illustrated here?

2.   What provides the necessary force for this process?

3.   What is the source of this force?

4.   How are molecules transported across the cell membrane?

5.   What substances are transported by this mechanism?

E.   Answer these questions concerning active transport. (p. 63)
1.   In active transport, molecules move from regions of_____ concentration to regions of
      _____ concentration.
2.   Compare active transport and facilitated diffusion.

F.   Answer the questions concerning the accompanying diagram. (p. 64)

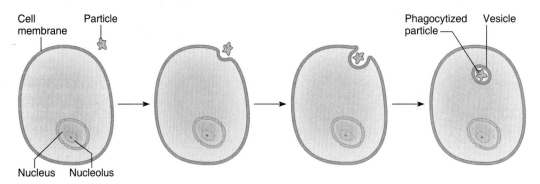

1.   What mechanism is illustrated in this drawing?

2.   What organelles are involved?

3.   What kinds of foreign objects are transported? Include pinocytosis, phagocytosis, and receptor mediated endocytosis in your answer.

4.   How is this mechanism important to cell survival?

V.   **3.4 The Cell Cycle (pp. 66–71)**

A.   1.   The series of changes that a cell undergoes from its formation until its reproduction is called its _____ . (p. 66)

        2.   DNA is replicated during the _____ phase of interphase.

B.   Describe each of the following events in mitosis. Include the function of telomeres. (pp. 66–67)

        prophase

        metaphase

        anaphase

        telophase

C.   Describe the events of cytoplasmic division. (p. 67)

D.	Answer these questions concerning cell differentiation. (pp. 67–70)

1.	The process by which cells develop differences in structure and function is_____ .

2.	Compare a stem cell and a progenitorcell.

E.	Describe the process of apoptosis (p. 70)

## V.	Clinical Focus Question

How is knowledge of the mechanisms of cellular transport and cellular reproduction applied to the treatment of disease?

When you have finished the study activities to your satisfaction, retake the mastery test and compare your results with your initial attempt. If you are not satisfied with your performance, repeat the appropriate study activities.

CHAPTER   **4**
CELLULAR METABOLISM

OVERVIEW

This chapter deals with two basic cellular processes: the use of energy and the use of genetic information to control cell processes. Specifically, this chapter discusses how enzymes control cell metabolism, how energy is released and made available to the cell, and how carbohydrates, lipids, and proteins are metabolized (objectives 1–6). It also explains how genetic information is stored, how it is used to control cell processes, and how the cell changes when genetic information is altered (objectives 8–9).

An understanding of life processes at the cellular level is basic to understanding how life processes occur at more complex levels—as in the whole organism.

CHAPTER OBJECTIVES

After you have studied this chapter, you should be able to:

4.1   Introduction
        1.   Briefly explain the role of genes in cellular metabolism.
4.2   Metabolic Reactions
        2.   Define *anabolism* and *catabolism.*
4.3   Control of Metabolic Reactions
        3.   Explain how enzymes control metabolic reactions.
4.4   Energy for Metabolic Reactions
        4.   Explain how cellular respiration releases chemical energy.
        5.   Describe how energy becomes available for cellular activities.
4.5   Metabolic Pathways
        6.   Describe the general metabolic pathways of carbohydrates, lipids, and proteins.
4.6   Nucleic Acids
        7.   Explain how nucleic acid molecules (DNA and RNA) store and carry genetic information.
4.7   DNA Replication
        8.   Describe how DNA molecules replicate.
4.8   Protein Synthesis
        9.   Explain how genetic information controls cellular processes.

FOCUS QUESTION

How do cells carry on life processes?

MASTERY TEST

Now take the mastery test. Do not guess. As soon as you complete the test, correct it. Note your successes and failures so that you can read the chapter to meet your learning needs.

1.   The proteins that control the reactions of metabolism are

      a.   amino acids.   c.   enzymes.

      b.   catalysts.   d.   substrates.

2.   The metabolic process that synthesizes materials needed for cellular growth is called_____
      _____ .

3.   The metabolic process that breaks down complex molecules into simpler ones is called_____
      _____ .

4. The process by which two molecules are joined together to form a more complex molecule is called

    a.   dehydration synthesis.   c.   atomization.

    b.   chemical bonding.

5. Glycerol and fatty acids become bonded to form water and

    a.   cholesterol.   c.   fat molecules.

    b.   lard.   d.   wax.

6. Amino acid molecules are joined by a peptide bond to form water and _____ .

7. The process by which water is added to a complex molecule to break it down, as represented by the equation $C_{12}H_{22}O_{11} + H_2O = C_6H_{12}O_6 + C_6H_{12}O_6$, is called _____ .

8. Enzymes are composed of

    a.   lipids.   c.   proteins.

    b.   carbohydrates.   d.   inorganic salts.

9. A substance that decreases the amount of energy necessary to begin a chemical reaction is a(n) _____.

10. An enzyme acts only on a particular substance that is called a

    a.   binding site.   c.   complement.

    b.   substrate.   d.   histologue.

11. An enzyme's ability to recognize the substance upon which it will act seems to be based on

    a.   atomic weight.   c.   structural formula.

    b.   molecular shape.

12. The speed of an enzyme-controlled reaction depends upon the number of _____ and _____ molecules present and the_____ of the enzyme.

13. A substance needed to convert an inactive form of an enzyme to an active form is called a(n) _____.

14. The form of energy utilized by most cellular processes is

    a.   chemical.   c.   thermal.

    b.   electrical.   d.   mechanical.

15. The process by which energy is released in the cell is called_____ .

16. The initial phase of respiration that occurs in the cytosol and produces two 3-carbon pyruvic acid molecules plus energy is called_____ _____ .

17. The second phase of respiration that occurs in the mitochondria and produces carbon dioxide, water, and energy is called _____ _____ .

18. What element is needed for this second phase to take place? _____

19. Name the storage place for the energy released by cellular respiration._____

20. A particular sequence of enzyme-controlled reactions is called a(n)_____ _____ .

21. We inherit traits from our parents because

    a.   DNA contains genes that are the carriers of inheritance.   c.   our species, *Homo sapiens,* reproduces sexually.

    b.   genes tell the cells to construct protein in a unique way for each individual.

22. A molecule consisting of a double spiral with sugar and phosphates forming the outer strands and organic bases joining the two strands is _____ .

23. List the four organic bases of DNA nucleotides.

24. DNA molecules are located in the_____ . Protein synthesis takes place in the_____ .

25. Two types of RNA are _____ RNA and_____ RNA.

26. In a molecule of RNA, the thymine nucleotide of DNA is replaced by _____ .

27.   The function of RNA is to

    a.   form lipids, such as cholesterol.   c.   control the bonding of amino acids.

    b.   guide the breakdown of polysaccharides.

28.   When the genetic material of a cell is altered, the result may be a(n)_____ .

29.   The rate at which a metabolic pathway functions is determined by a(n)_____
_____ that is present in limited quantity.

30.   Proteomics is the study of

    a.   protein synthesis   c.   protein conservation

    b.   gene reproduction   d.   gene expression

31.   DNA replication takes place during the _____ of the cell cycle.

STUDY ACTIVITIES

I.   Aids to Understanding Words

Define the following word parts. (p. 75)

an-   mut-

ana-   -zym

cata-

II.   4.1 Introduction (p. 75)

A.   Life is maintained by a series of_____ reactions.

B.   The reactions are controlled by proteins called _____.

III.   4.2 Metabolic Reactions (pp. 75–76)

A.   Answer these questions concerning anabolic metabolism. (p. 75)

    1.   Define *anabolic metabolism.*

    2.   The following formula is an example of anabolic metabolism. Label the formula, and identify the process
illustrated.

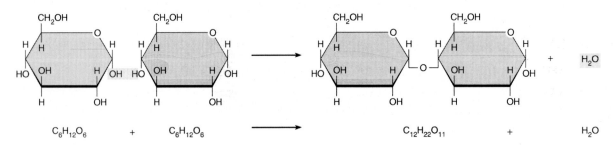

B.   Answer these questions concerning catabolism. (p. 75)

    1.   Define *catabolism.*

2. What process is illustrated here?

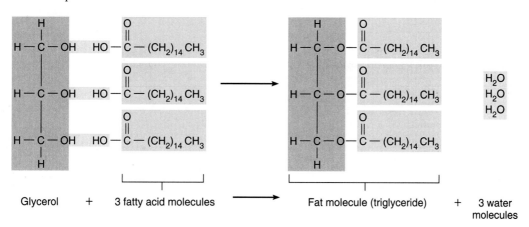

Glycerol   +   3 fatty acid molecules   ⟶   Fat molecule (triglyceride)   +   3 water molecules

IV.   4.3 Control of Metabolic Reactions (pp. 77–78)

A.   Enzymes promote chemical reactions in cells by _____ the amount of
_____ needed to initiate a reaction. (p. 77)

B.   What is the relationship between an enzyme and a substrate? Explain how this relationship works. (p. 77)

C.   What is a coenzyme? What substances are coenzymes? (p. 78)

D.   List the agents that can cause denaturization of enzymes. (p. 78)

V.   4.4 Energy for Metabolic Reactions (pp. 78–80)

A.   Answer these questions concerning energy and its release. (p. 78)

1.   What is energy?

2.   List six common forms of energy.

3.   The form of energy used by cell processes is _____ .

4.   This energy is released by the process of _____ .

B.   Fill in the following table, comparing aerobic and anaerobic respiration. (pp. 78–80)

Types of respiration

Type	Anaerobic	Aerobic
Location of reaction within cell		
How released energy is captured		
Number of molecules formed		

VI.   4.5 Metabolic Pathways (p. 80)

A.   What is a metabolic pathway? (p. 80)

B.   How are metabolic pathways regulated? (p. 80)

VII.   4.6 Nucleic Acids (pp. 80–82)

A.   What is a gene? (p. 80)

B.   How are genes necessary to cell metabolism?

C.   What is the genome? (p. 81)

D.   What is the structure of DNA? (pp. 81–82)

E.   What are the possible bases of nucleotides in DNA? (p. 82)

F.   Draw the matching strand of DNA for the strand illustrated here.

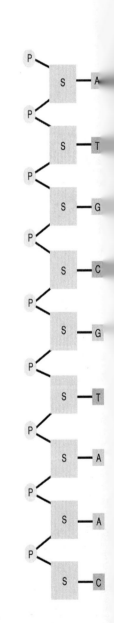

VIII.   **DNA-Replication (p. 82)**

A.   DNA molecules are replicated during _____ of the cell cycle.

B.   Explain the process of DNA replication.

IX.   **4.7 Protein Synthesis (pp. 82–86)**

A.   Where does protein synthesis occur? (pp. 82–84)

B.   How does RNA differ from DNA? (p. 84)

C.   Describe the roles of messenger RNA and transfer RNA in protein synthesis. (pp. 84–86)

D.   What is proteomics?

X. Clinical Focus Question

How do an individual's health history, past medical history, and medication history assist a health care professional in planning an individual's health care?

When you have finished the study activities to your satisfaction, retake the mastery test and compare your results with your initial attempt. If you are not satisfied with your performance, repeat the appropriate study activities.

CHAPTER 5
TISSUES

OVERVIEW

This chapter deals with the simplest level of organization of cells—tissues. It explains the types of tissue that occur in the human body, the general functions of each of these types of tissue, and the organs in which the various types of tissue and membranes occur (objectives 1–10).

The characteristics of a tissue remain the same regardless of where it occurs in the body. Knowledge of these characteristics is basic to understanding how a specific tissue contributes to the function of an organ.

CHAPTER OBJECTIVES

After you have studied this chapter, you should be able to:

5.1   Introduction
  1.   List the four major tissue types, and provide examples of where each occurs in the body.
5.2   Epithelial tissues
  2.   Describe the general characteristics and functions of epithelial tissue.
  3.   Name the types of epithelium, and identify an organ in which each is found.
  4.   Explain how glands are classified.
5.3   Connective tissues
  5.   List the types of connective tissues within the body.
  6.   Describe the general cellular components, structures, fibers, and matrix of each type of connective tissue.
  7.   Describe the major functions of each type of connective tissue.
5.4   Muscle tissues
  8.   Distinguish among the three types of muscle tissues.
5.5   Nervous tissues
  9.   Describe the general characteristics and functions of nervous tissue.
5.6   Types of membranes
  10.   Describe the four major types of membranes.

FOCUS QUESTION

How is tissue related to the organization of the body?

MASTERY TEST

Now take the mastery test. Do not guess. As soon as you complete the test, correct it. Note your successes and failures so that you can read the chapter to meet your learning needs.

1.   List the four major types of tissue found in the human body.
2.   Cells in a tissue are (similar, dissimilar).
3.   The function of epithelial tissue is to
  a.   support body parts.
  b.   cover body surfaces.
  c.   bind body parts together.
  d.   form the framework of organs.

4. Which of the following statements about epithelial tissue is(are) true?

    a. Epithelial tissue has no blood vessels.

    b. Epithelial cells reproduce slowly.

    c. Epithelial cells are nourished by substances diffusing from connective tissue.

    d. Injuries to epithelial tissue heal rapidly as new cells replace damaged cells.

5. Match the following types of epithelial cells with their correct location.

    _____ a. simple squamous epithelium   1. lining of the ducts of salivary glands

    _____ b. simple cuboidal epithelium   2. lining of respiratory passages

    _____ c. simple columnar epithelium   3. epidermis of the skin

    _____ d. pseudostratified columnar epithelium   4. air sacs of lungs, walls of capillaries

    _____ e. stratified squamous epithelium   5. lining of digestive tract

6. The inner lining of the urinary bladder and the passageways of the urinary tract are composed of
_____ _____ .

7. A gland that secretes its products into ducts opening into an external or internal surface is called
a(n) _____ gland.

8. A merocrine gland secretion that is thin, watery, and contains high concentrations of enzymes is called
_____ fluid.

9. The function of connective tissue is

    a. support.   c. coverage.

    b. protection.   d. fat storage.

10. Fibroblasts and mast cells found in connective tissue are (fixed/wandering) cells.

11. The connective tissue cells that produce fibers are:

    a. mast cells   c. fibroblasts

    b. macrophages

12. The major structural protein of the body and of white connective tissue is _____ .

13. Yellow connective tissue that can be stretched and returned to its original shape is _____ .

14. Which of the following statements is(are) true of loose connective tissue?

    a. It forms heavy, tough membranes under the skin and between muscles.

    b. It contains both yellow and white fibers.

    c. It has a meager blood supply.

    d. It contains few fibroblasts.

15. Which of the following statements is(are) true about adipose tissue?

    a. It is a specialized form of loose connective tissue.

    b. It occurs around the kidneys, behind the eyeballs, and around various joints.

    c. It serves as a conserver of body heat.

    d. It serves as a storehouse of energy for the body.

16. The cartilage found in the tip of the nose is _____ cartilage.

17. The type of cartilage in the intervertebral discs is _____ .

18. Because of the nature of its blood supply, injured cartilage heals (quickly, slowly).

19. The most rigid connective tissue is _____ .

20. The intercellular material of vascular tissue is _____ .

21. The three types of muscle tissue are _____, _____, and _____ .

22. Coordination and regulation of body functions is the function of _____ tissue.

23. Two or more kinds of tissue that work together to perform a specialized function make up a(n) _____ .

24. List the four major types of membranes.

25.   Serous membranes are located
        a. around the structures of the dorsal cavity
        b. in body cavities that are completely closed to the outside of the body
        c. wherever two bones come together

26.   Mucous membranes are located
        a. around the organs of the respiratory system
        b. in areas where two surfaces meet
        c. in the lining of cavities and tubes that have openings to the outside of the body

STUDY ACTIVITIES

I. Aids to Understanding Words

Define the following word and word parts. (p. 92)

adip-   macr-
chondr-   os-
-cyt   pseud-
epi-   squam-
-glia   strat-
inter-

II.   5.1 Introduction (p. 92)

A.   What are tissues? (p. 92)

B.   List the major tissue types and their functions.

C.   What is the matrix?

III.   5.2 Epithelial Tissues (pp. 92–98)

A.   List four functions of epithelial tissue. (p. 92)

B.   What is the function of the basement membrane? (p. 92)

C.   Answer these questions concerning simple squamous epithelium. (p. 93)
        1. The structure of simple squamous epithelium is _____ .
        2. Simple squamous epithelium is found where _____ and _____ take place.

D.   Answer these questions concerning simple cuboidal epithelium. (p. 93)
        1. Describe the structure of simple cuboidal epithelium.

        2. Where is this type of tissue found?

        3. The functions of simple cuboidal epithelium are_____ and _____ .

E.   Answer these questions concerning simple columnar epithelium. (pp. 93–94)

        1.   Describe the structure of simple columnar epithelium.

        2.   Where is this tissue located?

        3.   What is the function of simple columnar epithelium?

F.   Answer these questions concerning pseudostratified columnar epithelium. (pp. 94–95)

        1.   Microscopic, hairlike projections called _____ are a characteristic of columnar epithelium.

        2.   Where is this tissue found?

G.   Answer these questions concerning stratified squamous epithelium. (p. 95)

        1.   Describe the structure of stratified squamous epithelium.

        2.   Where is this tissue found?

H.   What is the special characteristic of transitional epithelium? (p. 95)

I.   Describe glandular epithelium. (p. 98)

J.   Fill in the following table. (p. 98)

Types of glandular secretions

Type of gland	Description of secretion	Examples
Merocrine		
Apocrine		
Holocrine		

IV.   5.3 Connective Tissues (pp. 99–105)

A.   What are the functions and structure of connective tissue? (p. 99)

B.   What are the functions of fibroblasts, macrophages, and mast cells? (p. 99)

C.   How do collagenous fibers and elastic fibers differ? (pp. 99–100)

D.   What is the difference between a ligament and a tendon? (p. 100)

E.   Where is adipose connective tissue found, and what is its function? (p. 101)

F.   Fill in the following table. (pp. 102–103)

Types of cartilage

Type	Location	Function
Hyaline		
Elastic		
Fibrocartilage		

G.   Answer these questions concerning bone. (pp. 103–104)
        1.   What are the characteristics of bone?

        2.   Bone injuries heal relatively rapidly. Why is this true?

H.   Answer these questions concerning blood (vascular connective tissue). (p. 105)
        1.   What is the intercellular material of vascular connective tissue?

        2.   What cells are found in the intercellular material?

        3.   Describe the functions of the connective tissue matrix.

V.   5.4 Muscle Tissues (pp. 105–108)

A.   What are the characteristics of muscle tissue? (p. 105)

B.   Fill in the following table. (pp. 105–108)

Muscle tissue

Type	Structure	Control	Location
Skeletal			
Smooth			
Cardiac			

VI. 5.5 Nervous Tissues (p. 108)

A.   What is the basic cell of nerve tissue?

B.   What is the function of neuroglial cells in nerve tissue?

C.   What is the function of nerve tissue?

VII. Types of Membranes (p. 109)

A.   List the three types of epithelial membranes.

B.   Where is each membrane found?

VIII. Clinical Focus Question

Kenny, age 10, is tall for his age, and his large muscles are well developed. He is very anxious to play football with a group of boys who are 14 and 15. What potential problems may result for Kenny? What tissues are most likely to be at risk for injury?

When you have finished the study activities to your satisfaction, retake the mastery test and compare your results with your initial attempt. If you are not satisfied with your performance, repeat the appropriate study activities.

## CHAPTER 6

SKIN AND THE INTEGUMENTARY SYSTEM

OVERVIEW

This chapter describes the skin and its accessory organs. It explains the structure and function of the layers of the skin (objectives 1, 2), skin color (objective 3), and the structure of hair, nails, and sweat glands (objective 4). It tells how the skin helps to regulate body temperature (objective 5). It describes the regulation of wound healing (objective 6).

Study of the integumentary system is essential to understanding how the body controls interaction between the internal and external environments.

CHAPTER OBJECTIVES

After you have studied this chapter, you should be able to:

6.1   Skin and Its Tissues

    1.   Describe the structure of layers of the skin.

    2.   List the general functions of each layer of skin.

    3.   Summarize the factors that determine skin color.

6.2   Accessory Organs of the Skin

    4.   Describe the accessory organs associated with the skin.

6.3   Regulation of Body Temperature

    5.   Explain how the skin helps regulate body temperature.

6.4   Healing of Wounds

    6.   Describe the events that are part of wound healing.

FOCUS QUESTION

How do the structure and function of the skin earn it the title of *the body's first line of defense?*

MASTERY TEST

Now take the mastery test. Do not guess. As soon as you complete the test, correct it. Note your successes and failures so that you can read the chapter to meet your learning needs.

1.   The outer layer of skin is called the _____.

2.   The inner layer of skin is called the _____.

3.   The masses of connective tissue beneath the inner layers of skin are called the _____
_____.

4.   The outer most layer of the epidermis is the

    a.   keratin.

    b.   stratum corneum.

    c.   stratum basale.

    d.   epidermis.

5.   The pigment that helps protect the deeper layers of the epidermis is

    a.   melanin.

    b.   trichosiderin.

    c.   biliverdin.

    d.   bilirubin.

6.   Light-complected, fair-haired people have (greater, fewer, equal) numbers of melanocytes than/as dark-complected, dark-haired people.

7.   Blood vessels supplying the skin are located in the _____.

8.   The subcutaneous layer functions as a(n) _____ _____.

9.   Smooth muscle cells that stand hairs on end in response to cold are known as _____ _____ _____.

10. The glands usually associated with hair follicles are
     a.   apocrine glands.   c.   sebaceous glands.
     b.   endocrine glands.   d.   exocrine glands.

11. Nails are produced by epidermal cells that undergo _____.

12. Where are the eccrine sweat glands most numerous?
     a.   the forehead   c.   the neck and back
     b.   the groin and the axilla   d.   evenly distributed over the body surface

13. The mammary glands of the breast that produce milk are modified _____ glands.

14. An irregularly shaped lesion with variegated color that develops on sun exposed areas is a(n) _____.

15. The sweat glands associated with regulation of body temperature are the
     a.   endocrine glands.   c.   exocrine glands.
     b.   eccrine glands.   d.   apocrine glands.

16. Which of the following organs produces the most heat?
     a.   kidneys   c.   muscles
     b.   bones   d.   lungs

17. Sponging the skin with water helps increase the loss of body heat by
     a.   evaporation.   c.   conduction.
     b.   convection.

18. Fibroblasts must migrate into a (shallow, deep) cut to heal the skin defect.

STUDY ACTIVITIES

I.   Aids to Understanding Words

Define the following word parts. (p. 112)

cut-   kerat-
derm-   melan-
epi-   seb-
follic-

II.   6.1 Skin and Its Tissues (pp. 113–116)

A.   List the components of the integumentary system. (p. 113)

B.   List the functions of the skin. (p. 113)

C.   What kinds of tissue are found in the skin? (p. 114)

D.   Label the layers of skin in the illustration below. (p. 114)

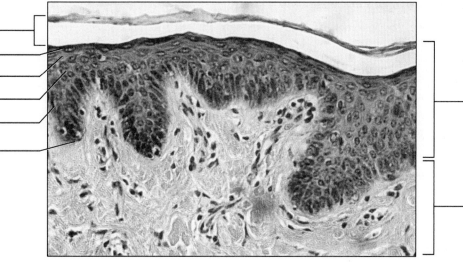

_____

_____

_____

_____

_____

© Victor B. Eichler

E.   Answer the following questions about the layers of the epidermis. (pp. 114–115)

    1.   What is the function of the stratum basale?

    2.   What is the function of the stratum corneum?

    3.   A callus or a corn is the result of a(n) _____ in cell reproduction in response to _____ or _____ .

F.   Deep layers of skin are protected from the ultraviolet portion of sunlight by _____. (p. 115)

G.   1.   What environmental factors influence skin color? (p. 116)

    2.   What physiologic factors influence skin color?

H.   Describe the structure and function of the dermis and the subcutaneous layer. (p. 116)

I.   Describe cutaneous carcinomas and cutaneous melanomas. (p. 119)

III. 6.2 Accessory Organs of the Skin (pp. 117–120)

A.   Where is the growing portion of the nail located? (p. 117)

B.   How is hair formed in this follicle? (pp. 117–118)

C.   Describe how hair responds to cold temperature or strong emotion. (p. 118)

D.   Where are sebaceous glands located, and what is the function of the substance they secrete? (p. 118)

E.   Label the following parts of a hair follicle on the illustration below: hair shaft, hair follicle, arrector pili muscle, sebaceous gland, blood vessels, dermis, epidermis, subcutaneous layer, sweat gland pore, stratum corneum, capillary, stratum basale, dermal papilla, basement membrane, touch receptor, sweat gland, sweat gland duct, nerve fiber, adipose cells. (p. 117)

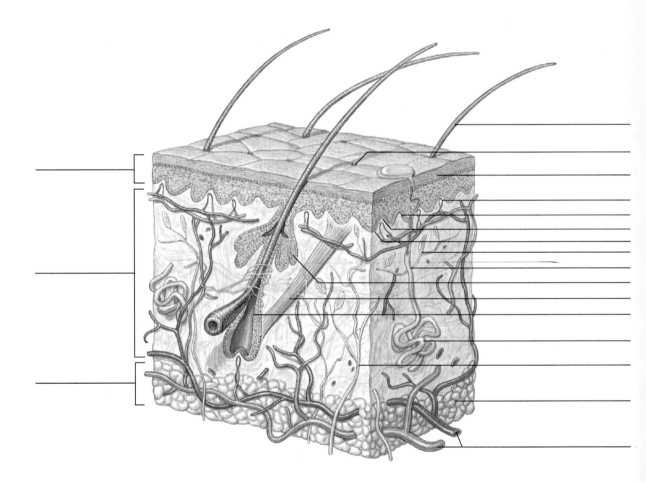

F.   Compare apocrine and eccrine sweat glands in relation to location, association with other skin structures, and activating stimuli. (pp. 118–120)

IV. 6.3 Regulation of Body Temperature (p. 120)

Describe the roles of the nervous, muscular, circulatory, and respiratory systems in heat regulation.

V. 6.4 Healing of Wounds (pp. 120–121)

A.   Describe the processes of inflammation. What function does this process serve? (p. 120)

B.   Compare healing of a shallow wound and a wound that extends into the dermis. (pp. 120–121)

VI. Clinical Focus Question

The ability to maintain body temperature is dependent on the integumentary system. Compare the integumentary systems of neonates and the elderly and identify the mechanisms that place these two age groups at risk for body temperature disturbances.

When you have finished the study activities to your satisfaction, retake the mastery test and compare your results with your initial attempt. If you are not satisfied with your performance, repeat the appropriate study activities.

OVERVIEW

This chapter deals with the skeletal system—the bones that form the framework for the body. It explains the function and structure of bones (objectives 1, 2, 4). The development of different types of bone is also explained (objective 3). The chapter describes skeletal organization and the location of specific bones within various parts of the skeleton (objectives 5 and 6). Various types of joints and the movements made possible by these joints (objectives 7–9) are also described in chapter 7.

Movement is a characteristic of living things. A study of the skeletal system is necessary to understand how complex organisms, such as humans, are organized to accomplish movement.

CHAPTER OBJECTIVES

After you have studied this chapter, you should be able to:

7.1   Introduction
   1.   List the active tissues in a bone.

7.2   Bone Structure
   2.   Describe the general structure of a bone, and list the functions of its parts.

7.3   Bone Development and Growth
   3.   Distinguish between intramembranous and endochondral bones, and explain how such bones develop and grow.

7.4   Bone Function
   4.   Discuss the major functions of bones.

7.5   Skeletal Organization
   5.   Distinguish between the axial and appendicular skeletons, and name the major parts of each.

7.6–7.12 Skull–Lower Limb
   6.   Locate and identify the bones and the major features of the bones that comprise the skull, vertebral column, thoracic cage, pectoral girdle, upper limb, pelvic girdle, and lower limb.

7.13   Joints
   7.   List three classes of joints, describe their characteristics, and name an example of each.
   8.   List six types of synovial joints, and describe the actions of each.
   9.   Explain how skeletal muscles produce movements at joints, and identify several types of joint movements.

FOCUS QUESTION

How do your bones and joints help you to get out of bed and to your anatomy and physiology class?

MASTERY TEST

Now take the mastery test. Do not guess. As soon as you complete the test, correct it. Note your successes and failures so that you can read the chapter to meet your learning needs.

1.   Which of the following is <u>not</u> an active tissue found in bone?

    a.   cartilage   c.   blood

    b.   cuboidal epithelium   d.   nervous tissue

2.   The shaft of a long bone is the

    a.   epiphysis.   b.   diaphysis.

3.   To what part of the bone do tendons and ligaments attach?

    a.   bursae   c.   cartilage

    b.   epiphysis   d.   periosteum

4.   Bone that consists mainly of tightly packed tissue is called _____.

5.   Bone that consists of numerous branching bony plates separated by irregular spaces is called _____.

6.   The medullary cavity of a long bone is filled with _____.

7.   Bones that develop from layers of membranous connective tissue are called_____

    _____.

8.   Bones that develop from masses of hyaline cartilage are called _____ _____.

9.   The band of cartilage between the primary and secondary ossification centers in long bones is called the

    a.   osteoblastic band.   c.   periosteal plate.

    b.   calcium disk.   d.   epiphyseal plate.

10.   The cells that form new bone are _____; the cells that break down bone are _____.

11.   Once bone formation is complete, the bone (remains stable, is remodeled) throughout life.

12.   When a bone is fractured, a hematoma is formed from blood escaping from

    a.   the periosteum.   c.   blood vessels within the bone.

    b.   bone marrow.   d.   surrounding soft tissue.

13.   The gap between broken ends of a fractured bone is filled by a _____ _____.

14.   To accomplish movement, bones and muscles function together to act as _____.

15.   Which of the following bones contain red marrow for blood cell formation in a healthy adult?

    a.   pelvis   c.   ribs

    b.   small bones of the wrist   d.   shaft of long bones

16.   Which of the following substances are NOT normally found in bone?

    a.   potassium   c.   lead

    b.   calcium   d.   magnesium

17.   The bones most often affected by osteoporosis are the

    a.   facial bones.   c.   bones of the skull.

    b.   hip bones.   d.   vertebrae.

18.   The hormone associated with the development of osteoporosis is

    a.   testosterone.   c.   progesterone.

    b.   estrogen.   d.   calcitonin.

19.   List the major parts of the axial skeleton.

20.   List the major parts of the appendicular skeleton.

21.   The part of the spinal column in which the vertebrae are fused is the

    a.   cervical spine   c.   sacrum

    b.   thoracic spine   d.   coccyx

22.   The only movable bone of the skull is the

    a.   nasal bone.   c.   maxilla.

    b.   mandible.   d.   vomer.

23. The bone that forms the back of the skull and joins the skull along the lamboidal suture is the _____ bone.

24. The upper jaw is formed by the _____ bones.

25. The membranous areas (soft spots) of an infant's skull are called _____.

26. What part of the vertebral column acts as a shock absorber?
    a. vertebral bodies
    b. intervertebral disks
    c. lamina
    d. spinous processes

27. Which of the vertebrae support the most weight?
    a. cervical
    b. thoracic
    c. lumbar
    d. sacral

28. The functions of the thoracic cage include
    a. production of blood cells.
    b. contribution to breathing.
    c. protection of heart and lungs.
    d. support of the shoulder girdle.

29. True ribs articulate with _____ _____ and the _____.

30. The pectoral girdle is made of two _____ and two _____.

31. The _____ crosses over the ulna when the palm of the hand faces backward.

32. The wrist consists of
    a. 8 carpal bones.
    b. 5 metacarpal bones.
    c. 14 phalanges.
    d. distal segments of the radius and the ulna.

33. When the hands are placed on the hips, they are placed over the
    a. iliac crest.
    b. acetabulum.
    c. ischial tuberosity.
    d. ischial spines.

34. The longest bone in the body is the
    a. tibia.
    b. fibula.
    c. femur.
    d. patella.

35. The lower end of the fibula can be felt as an ankle bone. The correct name is the
    a. head of the fibula.
    b. lateral malleolus.
    c. talus.
    d. lesser trochanter.

36. Synovial membrane is found in
    a. immovable joints.
    b. slightly movable joints.
    c. freely movable joints.

37. The function of bursae is to
    a. act as shock absorbers.
    b. facilitate movement of tendons over bones.
    c. reduce friction between bony surfaces.
    d. protect joints from infection.

38. The type of joint that permits the widest range of motion is
    a. ball-and-socket.
    b. gliding.
    c. condyloid.
    d. pivot.

39. Moving the parts at a joint so that the angle between them is increased is called
    a. flexion.
    b. extension.
    c. elevation.
    d. abduction.

STUDY ACTIVITIES

I. Aids to Understanding Words

Define the following word parts. (p. 126)

acetabul-

ax-

-blast

carp-

-clast

condyl-

corac-

cribr-

crist-

fov-

glen-

hema-

inter-

intra-

meat-

odont-

poie-

II. 7.1 Introduction (p. 126)

List the living tissues of bone. (p. 126)

III. 7.2 Bone Structure (pp. 126–127)

A. Label the following parts in the accompanying drawing of a long bone: diaphysis, articular cartilage, spongy bone, compact bone, medullary cavity, yellow marrow, periosteum, epiphyseal disks, proximal epiphysis, distal epiphysis, space occupied by red marrow.

B. How does the structure of bone make its function possible?

C. The vascular fibrous tissue covering the bone whose function is the formation and repair of bone tissue is the _____. (p. 126)

D. What is the structural difference between compact and spongy bone? (p. 126)

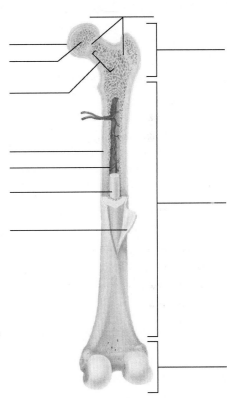

E. Osteocytes are found in the
   a.   central canals.
   b.   lacunae.
   c.   medullary cavity.
   d.   periosteum.

IV. 7.3 Bone Development and Growth (pp. 127–130)

A.   What bones are intramembranous bones? How do these develop? (pp. 127–128)

B.   What bones are endochondral bones? How do these develop? Be sure to include descriptions of the primary ossification center, the secondary ossification center, and the epiphyseal disk. (pp. 128–129)

C.   Answer these questions concerning ossification. (p. 129)
    1.   When is ossification complete?

    2.   Describe the homeostasis of bone tissue.

D.   How is the fracture of a bone healed? (p. 131)

V. 7.4 Bone Function (pp. 130–133)

A.   What bones function primarily to provide support? (p. 130)

B.   What bones function primarily to protect viscera? (p. 130)

C.   How do bones function with muscles to produce movement? (p. 130)

D.   Answer these questions concerning blood cell formation. (pp. 130–132)
    1.   Where are blood cells formed in the embryo? In the infant? In the adult?

    2.   What is the difference between red and yellow marrow?

Answer these questions concerning the inorganic compounds in bone. (pp. 132–133)

1. What are the major inorganic salts stored in bone? What other salts and heavy metals can also be stored in bone?

2. How is calcium released from bone so that it is available for physiologic processes?

3. What is osteoporosis?

VI. 7.5 Skeletal Organization (pp. 133–135)

A. What are the two major divisions of the skeleton? (p. 133)

B. List the bones found in each of these major divisions. (pp. 133–135)

VII. 7.6 Skull (pp. 136–141)

A. Answer these questions concerning the number of bones in the skull. (p. 136)
  1. How many bones are found in the human skull?
  2. How many of these bones are found in the cranium?
  3. How many are found in the facial skeleton?

B. Answer these questions concerning the cranial bones. (pp. 136–139)
  1. Using your own head or that of a partner, locate the following cranial bones and identify the suture lines that form their boundaries: occipital bone, temporal bones, frontal bones, and parietal bones.
  2. What are the remaining two bones of the cranium? Where are they located?

C. Answer these questions concerning the facial bones. (pp. 140–141)
  1. Using yourself or a partner, locate the following facial bones: maxilla, palatine, zygomatic, lacrimal bones, nasal bones, vomer, inferior nasal conchae, and mandible.
  2. Which of the facial bones is the only movable bone of the skull?

  3. Describe the differences between the infant and the adult skull.

VIII.   7.7 Vertebral Column (pp. 141–145)

A.   What is the function of the vertebral column? Of intervertebral disks? (p. 141)

B.   Label the following parts of the accompanying diagram: lamina, transverse process, pedicle, superior articulating process, body, vertebral foramen. (p. 143)

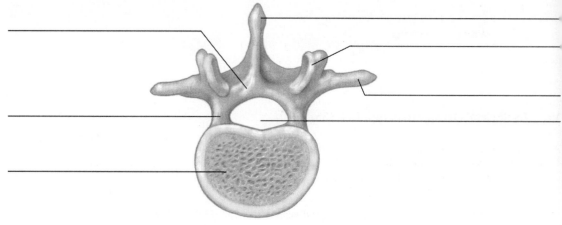

Lumbar vertebra

C.   In what ways is the structure of the thoracic vertebrae unique? (p. 143)

D.   In what ways is the structure of the lumbar vertebrae unique? (p. 143)

E.   Locate the sacrum and the coccyx. (pp. 143–145)

IX.   7.8 Thoracic Cage (p.145)

A.   Name the bones of the thoracic cage. (p. 145)

B.   Describe the differences between true and false ribs. (p. 145)

C.   Describe the sternum, including the manubrium, body, and xiphoid process. Locate these structures on yourself. (p. 145)

X.   7.9 Pectoral Girdle (p. 146)

Using yourself or a partner, locate and list the bones of the pectoral girdle. What is the function of the pectoral girdle?

XI.   7.10 Upper Limb (pp. 146–149)

A.   Using yourself or a partner, locate and list the bones of the upper limb.

B.   Label the following parts in the drawing below: phalanges, metacarpals, carpals, pisiform, triquetrum, hamate, lunate, capitate, scaphoid, trapezoid, trapezium, radius, ulna, proximal phalanx, middle phalanx, distal phalanx. (p. 151)

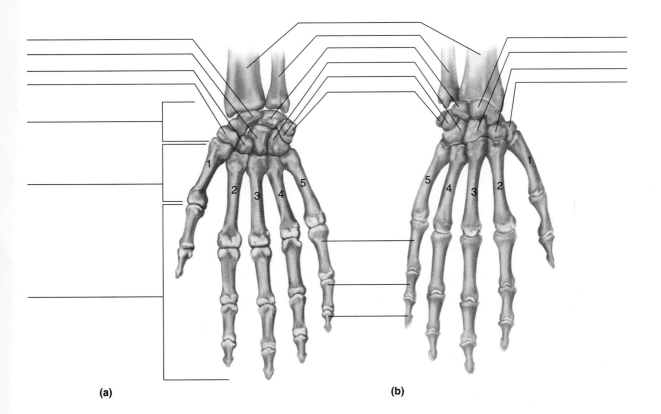

(a)   (b)

XII.   7.11 Pelvic Girdle (pp. 150–151)

A.   List the bones of the pelvic girdle. (p. 150)

B.   Identify the bone in which each of the following structures is located, and explain the function of each structure. (pp. 150–152)

Structure and function of bones of the pelvic girdle

Structure	Bone	Function
Acetabulum		
Anterior superior iliac spine		
Ischial spine		
Obturator foramen		

XIII.   7.12 Lower Limb (pp. 152–154)

A.   List the bones of the lower limb. (p. 154)

B.   Identify the bone in which each of the following structures is located, and explain the function of each structure. (pp. 152–154)

Structure and function of bones of the lower limb

Structure	Bone	Function
Fovea capitis		
Medial malleolus		
Lateral malleolus		
Greater and lesser trochanters		
Tibial tuberosity		

C.   Label these structures on the accompanying illustration: tarsal bones, calcaneus, talus, metatarsals, phalanges, navicular, cuboid, lateral cuneiform, intermediate cuneiform, medial cuneiform, proximal phalanx, middle phalanx, distal phalanx. (p. 156)

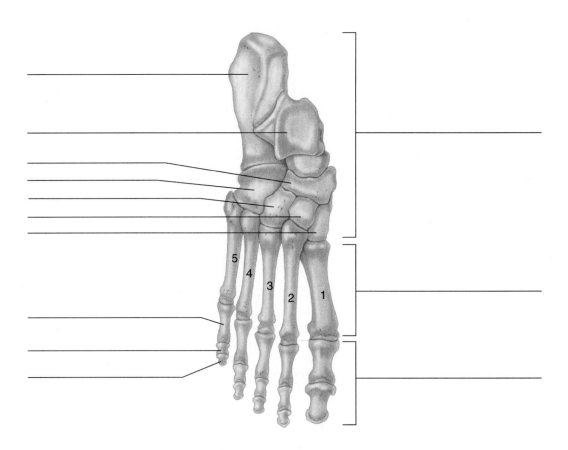

7.13 Joints (pp. 154–157)

..   Describe and give an example of each of the following types of joints. (pp. 154–157)

The joints

Joint	Description	Example
Fibrous joint		
Cartilaginous joint		
Synovial joint		
Ball-and-socket joint		
Condyloid joint		
Gliding joint		
Hinge joint		
Pivot joint		
Saddle joint		

B.   Describe the structure and function of a synovial joint. (pp. 155–157)

C.   Identify the following movements. (pp. 157–159)
            turning the palms of the hands upward
            shrugging the shoulders
            bending the arm at the elbow
            reaching for an object that is just beyond one's reach
            turning the hands down so the palms face the floor
            moving the legs apart in an "at ease" position
            moving the legs together in an "attention" position
            swiveling the head
            drawing a large circle on the blackboard

XV. Clinical Focus Question

Describe a lifestyle that may prevent the development of osteoporosis. Include the following:

1.   genetic endowment.
2.   nutrition.
3.   activity.
4.   growth and development.
5.   health education.

When you have finished the study activities to your satisfaction, retake the mastery test and compare your results with your initial attempt. If you are not satisfied with your performance, repeat the appropriate study activities.

OVERVIEW

In conjunction with the skeletal system, the muscular system serves to move the body. This chapter introduces the three types of muscle; the major events in contraction of skeletal, smooth, and cardiac muscles; the energy supply to muscle fiber for contraction; the occurrence of oxygen debt; and the process of muscle fatigue (objectives 4, 5, 6). This chapter also describes the structure and function of a skeletal muscle; distinguishes between a twitch and a sustained contraction; explains how various kinds of muscle contraction produce body movements and maintain posture; shows how the location and interaction of muscles produce body movements; identifies the location and action of major skeletal muscles; and differentiates the structure and function of a multiunit smooth muscle and a visceral smooth muscle (objectives 1, 2, 3, 7, 8, 9, 10, 11, 12, 13).

The skeletal system can be thought of as the passive partner in producing movement: think of the muscular system as the active partner. This chapter explains how muscles interact with bones to maintain posture and produce movement. In addition, it tells the characteristics and functions of skeletal, smooth, and cardiac muscles. This knowledge is a foundation for the study of other organ systems, such as the digestive, respiratory, and cardiovascular systems.

CHAPTER OBJECTIVES

After you have studied this chapter, you should be able to:

8.1   Introduction

1. List various outcomes of muscular actions.

8.2   Structure of a Skeletal Muscle

2. Describe how connective tissue is part of a skeletal muscle.

3. Name the major parts of a skeletal muscle fiber, and describe the function of each.

8.3   Skeletal Muscle Contraction

4. Explain the major events of skeletal muscle fiber contraction.

5. Explain how the muscle fiber contraction mechanism obtains energy.

6. Describe how oxygen debt develops and how a muscle may become fatigued.

8.4   Muscular Responses

7. Distinguish between a twitch and a sustained contraction.

8. Explain how the types of muscular contractions produce body movements and help maintain posture.

8.5   Smooth Muscles

9. Distinguish between the structures and functions of a multiunit smooth muscle and a visceral smooth muscle.

10. Compare the contraction mechanisms of skeletal and smooth muscle fibers.

8.6   Cardiac Muscle

11. Compare the contraction mechanism of skeletal and cardiac muscle fibers.

8.7   Skeletal Muscle Actions

12. Explain how the locations and interactions of skeletal muscles are related to the movements they produce and describe how muscles interact to produce such movements.

13. Describe the locations and actions of the major skeletal muscles of each body region.

FOCUS QUESTION

How do muscle cells use energy and interact with bones to get you from your anatomy and physiology classroom to track team practice?

MASTERY TEST

Now take the mastery test. Do not guess. As soon as you complete the test, correct it. Note your successes and failures so that you can read the chapter to meet your learning needs.

1. The kind of energy that muscles use to contract is
   - a. chemical
   - b. electrical
   - c. heat

2. List the tissues found in skeletal muscle.

3. An individual skeletal muscle is separated from adjacent muscles by _____.

4. Layers of connective tissue extending into the muscle to form partitions between muscle bundles are continuous with attachments of muscle to periosteum called
   - a. ligaments.
   - b. tendons.
   - c. aponeuroses.
   - d. elastin.

5. The characteristic striated appearance of skeletal muscle is due to the arrangement of alternating protein filaments composed of _____ and _____ .

6. An injury in which a few muscle fibers are torn but the fascia is left intact is called a _____ _____ _____ .

7. The union between a nerve fiber and a muscle fiber is the
   - a. motor neuron.
   - b. motor end plate.
   - c. neuromuscular junction.
   - d. neurotransmitter.

8. A motor neuron and the muscle fibers it controls are called a _____ _____.

9. When the cross-bridge of the myosin molecule forms linkages with actin filaments, the result is
   - a. shortening of the muscle fiber.
   - b. membrane polarization.
   - c. release of acetylcholine.

10. The chemical that is necessary for the transmission of an impulse from a nerve to a muscle fiber is _____.

11. The energy used in muscle contraction is supplied by the decomposition of _____ _____.

12. A substance that stores energy released when stores of the substance in number 10 are in low supply is
   _____ _____.

13. The ion necessary to link myosin and actin is
   - a. sodium.
   - b. calcium.
   - c. magnesium.
   - d. potassium.

14. A person feels out of breath after vigorous exercise because of oxygen debt. Which of the following statements helps explain this phenomenon?
   - a. Anaerobic respiration increases during strenuous activity.
   - b. Lactic acid is metabolized more efficiently when the body is at rest.
   - c. Conversion of lactic acid to glycogen occurs in the liver and requires energy.
   - d. Priority in energy use is given to ATP synthesis.

15. After prolonged muscle use, muscle fatigue occurs due to an accumulation of _____ _____.

16. The minimal strength stimulus needed to elicit contraction of a single muscle fiber is called a(n) _____ _____.

17. The strength of a muscle contraction in response to different levels of stimulation is determined by the
   - a. level of stimulation delivered to individual muscle fibers.
   - b. number of fibers that respond in each motor unit.
   - c. number of motor units stimulated.
   - d. characteristics of each muscle group.

18. The period of time between a stimulus to a muscle and muscle response is called the
   - a. latent period.
   - b. contraction.
   - c. refractory period.

9. Muscle tone refers to

    a. a state of sustained, partial contraction of muscles that is necessary to maintain posture.

    b. a feeling of well-being following exercise.

    c. the ability of a muscle to maintain contraction against an outside force.

    d. the condition athletes attain after intensive training.

20. Atrophy refers to a(n) (increase, decrease) in the size and strength of a muscle.

21. Two types of smooth muscle are _____ muscle and _____ muscle.

22. Peristalsis is due to which of the following characteristics of smooth muscle?

    a. capacity of smooth muscle fibers to excite each other

    b. automaticity

    c. rhythmicity

    d. sympathetic innervation

23. Smooth muscle contracts (more slowly, more rapidly) than skeletal muscle following stimulation.

24. Impulses travel relatively (rapidly, slowly) through cardiac muscle.

25. The attachment of a muscle to a relatively fixed part is called the _____; the attachment to a relatively movable part is called the _____.

26. Smooth body movements depend on _____ giving way to prime movers.

27. The muscle that compresses the cheeks inward when it contracts is the

    a. orbicularis oris.

    b. epicranius.

    c. platysma.

    d. buccinator.

28. The muscle that moves the head to one side is the

    a. sternocleidomastoid.

    b. splenius capitis.

    c. semispinalis capitis.

    d. longissimus capitis.

29. The muscle that abducts the upper arm and can both flex and extend the humerus is the

    a. biceps brachii.

    b. deltoid.

    c. infraspinatus.

    d. triceps brachii.

30. The band of tough connective tissue that extends from the xiphoid process to the symphysis pubis and serves as an attachment for muscles of the abdominal wall is the _____ _____.

31. The heaviest muscle in the body, which serves to straighten the leg at the hip during walking, is the

    a. psoas major.

    b. gluteus maximus.

    c. adductor longus.

    d. gracilis.

STUDY ACTIVITIES

I. Aids to Understanding Words

Define the following word parts. (p. 169)

calat-

erg-

hyper-

inter-

laten-

myo-

sarco-

syn-

tetan-

-troph

II. 8.1 Introduction (p. 169)

List the three types of muscle. (p. 169)

III. 8.2 Structure of a Skeletal Muscle (pp. 169–172)

A.   List the kinds of tissue present in skeletal muscle. (p. 169)

B.   Answer these questions concerning skeletal muscle tissues. (p. 169)

      1.   A skeletal muscle is held in position by layers of fibrous connective tissue called _____.

      2.   This tissue extends beyond the end of a skeletal muscle to form a cordlike _____.

      3.   When this tissue extends beyond the muscle to form a sheetlike structure, it is called a(n) _____.

      4.   What are fascicles?

C.   Answer these questions concerning skeletal muscle fibers. (p. 169)

      1.   Describe a single muscle fiber (pp. 169–172)

      2.   Describe the structure and function of a sarcomere.

      3.   The network of membranous channels in the cytoplasm of muscle fibers is the _____ _____. The other channels found in the cytoplasm are the _____ _____.

      4.   What is the function of these channels?

D.   Label these structures in the accompanying illustration of a neuromuscular junction: mitochondria, synaptic cleft, synaptic vesicles, folded sarcolemma, muscle fiber nucleus, myofibril of muscle fiber, motor end plate, (2) axon branches, motor neuron axon.

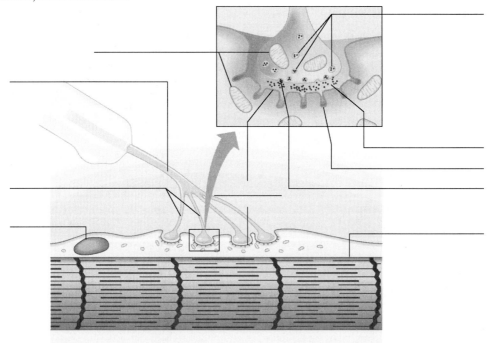

IV. 8.3 Skeletal Muscle Contraction (pp. 173–177)

A.   Describe the roles of actin and myosin in muscle contraction. (p. 173)

B.   Describe the transmission of a nerve impulse across the neuromuscular junction. (p. 173)

C.   Answer these questions concerning stimulus for contraction. (pp. 173–175)
        1.   Describe the interaction of acetylcholine and calcium ions in stimulating muscle contraction.

        2.   What is a cross-bridge?

        3.   The action of acetylcholine is halted by the enzyme _____.

D.   Answer these questions concerning energy sources for contraction. (pp. 175–176)
        1.   How does ATP supply energy for muscle contraction?

        2.   How does creatine phosphate supply energy for muscle contraction?

E.   Answer these questions concerning oxygen supply and cellular respiration. (p. 176)
        1.   What substance in muscle seems able to store oxygen temporarily?

        2.   Why is oxygen necessary for muscle contraction?

        3.   How does the muscle continue to contract in the absence of oxygen?

        4.   What is meant by oxygen debt?

F.   Answer these questions concerning muscle fatigue. (p. 177)
        1.   What is meant by muscle fatigue? What causes it?

        2.   Less than half the energy released by cellular respiration is available for metabolic processes. The rest is lost as
                _____.

V.   8.4 Muscular Responses (pp. 177–180)

A.   Answer these questions concerning muscular responses. (pp. 177–180)
        1.   Define *threshold stimulus*.

        2.   Define *all-or-none response*.

        3.   Describe summation.

4. Describe recruitment.

B. The accompanying illustration shows a myogram of a type of muscle contraction known as a twitch. Label the following: time of stimulation, latent period, period of contraction, period of relaxation. Explain the significance of each of these events. (p. 179)

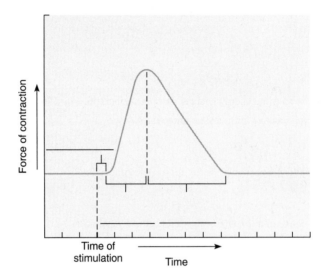

C. Describe the role of slow muscle fibers and fast muscle fibers in the response of a muscle to different types of exercise. (p. 180)

D. Describe these kinds of muscle contractions. (p. 180)
    sustained contraction

    muscle tone

VI. 8.5 Smooth Muscles (p. 181)

A. Compare the structure of smooth muscle fibers and skeletal muscle fibers. (p. 181)

B. Answer these questions about smooth muscle. (p. 181)
    1. The two types of smooth muscle are _____ smooth muscle and _____ smooth muscle.
    2. Where are each of these types of smooth muscle found?

    3. The properties of smooth muscle that allows peristalsis are _____ and _____.

C. Answer these questions about smooth muscle contraction. (p. 181)
    1. The neurotransmitters that affect smooth muscle are_____ and _____.
    2. Do these neurotransmitters always lead to muscle contraction?
    3. Compare the characteristics of smooth muscle contraction and skeletal contraction.

4. Match the following descriptions with the genetic diseases they describe. (p. 183)

_____a. muscular dystrophies

1. Delayed muscle relation following contraction in which the symptoms become increasingly severe in successive generations.

_____b. Charcot-Marie-Tooth Disease

2. A genetic error that leads to the change of a single DNA nucleotide base leading to a defect in the ability of actin to anchor to Z bands.

_____c. myotonic dystrophy

3. Muscles that weaken and degenerate due to abnormalities of the protein dystrophin.

_____d. hereditary idiopathic dilated cardiomyopathy

4. Characterized by progressing weakness in the muscles of the hands and feet diagnosed by electromyography and nerve conduction velocity studies.

VII. 8.6 Cardiac Muscle (pp. 181–182)

A. Describe the structure of the sarcoplasmic reticulum of cardiac muscle and the effect of this structure on cardiac muscle contraction. (p. 181)

B. Opposing ends of cardiac muscle fibers are connected by_____ - _____
_____. (p. 181)

C. Describe the effect of the properties of self-excitation and rhythmicity and cardiac muscle contraction. (pp. 181–182)

VIII. 8.7 Skeletal Muscle Actions (pp. 182–184)

A. A skeletal muscle has at least two places of attachment to bone. For instance, the gluteus maximus, which extends the leg at the hip, is attached to the posterior surface of the ilium, the sacrum, and the coccyx at one end and to the posterior surface of the femur and the iliotibial tract at the other. One place of muscle attachment is the origin, and the other is the insertion. Explain the difference between the two. (p. 182)

B. Match the terms in the first column with the statements in the second column that best describe the role of muscle groups in producing smooth muscle movement. (p. 184)

_____1. prime mover

_____2. synergist

_____3. antagonist

a. muscle that returns a part to its original position

b. muscle that makes the action of the prime mover more effective

c. muscle that has the major responsibility for producing a movement

C. Define *flexion* and *extension*. (pp. 182–184)

IX. Clinical Focus Question

You are a school nurse in a high school known for the excellence of its athletic programs. You have been asked by the board of education to address the issue of steroid use by male and female athletes. In preparing your statement, you must address the following issues:

1. Why do athletes use steroid drugs?

2. What kind of testing program can be implemented to ensure students in this school are not using such drugs?

3. What are the symptoms of steroid use in males and females?

4.   What problems are associated with use of these drugs?

When you have finished the study activities to your satisfaction, retake the mastery test and compare your results with your initial attempt. If you are not satisfied with your performance, repeat the appropriate study activities.

OVERVIEW

The human body depends on the nervous system and the endocrine system to coordinate and integrate the functions of other body systems so that the internal environment remains able to function normally. The chapter focuses on the nervous system. The structure and function of the various parts of the nervous system and its various tissues is the foundation for your understanding of the nervous system (objectives 1–6). You will learn how neurons of various types are classified and function (objectives 7–11). The processing of information is discussed (objective 12) as well as the functions of the various tissues, organs, and divisions of the nervous system (objectives 12–20).

CHAPTER OBJECTIVES

After you have studied this chapter, you should be able to:

9.1   Introduction
      1. Distinguish between the two groups of cells that comprise the nervous system.
      2. Name the two major groups of nervous system organs.

9.2   General Functions of the Nervous System
      3. Explain the general functions of the nervous system.

9.3   Neuroglial Cells
      4. State the functions of neuroglial cells in the central nervous system.
      5. Distinguish among the types of neuroglial cells in the central nervous system.
      6. Describe the Schwann cells of the peripheral nervous system.

9.4   Neurons
      7. Describe the general structure of a neuron.
      8. Explain how differences in structure and function are used to classify neurons.

9.5   Cell Membrane Potential
      9. Explain how a membrane becomes polarized.

9.6   Nerve Impulse
      10. Describe the events that lead to the conduction of a nerve impulse.

9.7   The Synapse
      11. Explain how information passes from one neuron to another.

9.8   Impulse Processing
      12. Describe the general ways in which the nervous system processes information.

9.9   Types of Nerves
      13. Describe how nerve fibers in peripheral nerves are classified.

9.10   Nerve Pathways
      14. Name the parts of a reflex arc, and describe the function of each part.

9.11   Meninges
      15. Describe the coverings of the brain and spinal cord.

9.12   Spinal Cord

      16. Describe the structure of the spinal cord and its major functions.

9.13   Brain

      17. Name the major parts and functions of the brain.

      18. Distinguish among motor, sensory, and association areas of the cerebral cortex.

      19. Describe the formation and function of cerebrospinal fluid.

9.14   Peripheral Nervous System

      20. List the major parts of the peripheral nervous system.

      21. Name the cranial nerves, and list their major functions.

      22. Describe the structure of a spinal nerve.

9.15   Autonomic Nervous System

      23. Describe the functions of the autonomic nervous system.

      24. Distinguish between the sympathetic and parasympathetic divisions of the autonomic nervous system.

      25. Describe a sympathetic and a parasympathetic nerve pathway.

FOCUS QUESTION

It is noon, and you are just finishing an anatomy assignment. You hear your stomach growling and realize you are hungry. You make a ham sandwich and pour a glass of milk. After you finish eating, you realize you have been studying for three hours and should go for a walk. How does the nervous system receive internal and external cues, process incoming information, and decide what action to take?

MASTERY TEST

Now take the mastery test. Do not guess. As soon as you complete the test, correct it. Note your successes and failures so that you can read the chapter to meet your learning needs.

1.   The basic unit of structure and function of the nervous system is the _____.

2-5.   Match the function listed in Column A with the structure in Column B.

Function		**Structure**
a. information transmitted in the form of electrical and chemical changes	2.	axon
b. extension of neuron cell body	3.	nerve impulse
c. receives information as electochemical messages	4.	nerve fiber
d. sends information	5.	dendrite

6.   The three general functions of the peripheral nervous system are _____, _____, and _____.

7.   The motor functions of the nervous system that are consciously controlled are part of the _____ nervous system.

8.   The supporting cells of the central nervous system are _____ cells.

9.   The type of neuroglial cells found between neurons and blood vessels that join parts by numerous cellular processes are

     a.   microglial cells.   c.   astrocytes.

     b.   oligodendrocytes.   d.   ependymal cells.

10.   Does statement *a* explain statement *b*? _____.

     a.   The nucleus of the nerve cell seems incapable of mitosis.

     b.   The nerve cell cannot reproduce.

11.   The neurilemma is composed of

     a.   Nissl bodies.   c.   the cytoplasm and nuclei of Schwann cells.

     b.   myelin.   d.   neuron cell bodies.

12.   Axons arise from a part of the cell body known as the _____ _____.

13. List the major groups of neurons classified on the basis of structure.

14. Neurons may be classified functionally as _____, _____, and _____ neurons.

15. When the nerve cell is at rest, the concentration of _____ ions is relatively greater on the outside of the cell membrane.

16. When the threshold potential is reached, the region of the cell membrane being stimulated undergoes a change in _____.

17. Nerves with _____ diameters conduct impulses faster than those with _____ diameters.

18. The junction between two communicating neurons is called a(n) _____.

19. Transmission of nerve impulses from one neuron to another is controlled by substances called _____.

20. The function of neuronal pools is _____ of nerve impulses.

21. Divergence occurs when

    a. an impulse is amplified.

    b. an additive effect is noted.

    c. an impulse reaches different regions of the brain.

    d. nerve fibers divide.

22. A bundle of nerve fibers held together by connective tissue is a(n) _____.

23. An automatic, unconscious response to a change inside or outside the body is a(n) _____.

24. The organs of the central nervous system are the _____ and the _____.

25. The outer membrane covering the brain is composed of fibrous connective tissues and is called the

    a. dura mater.

    b. arachnoid mater.

    c. pia mater.

    d. periosteum.

26. Cerebrospinal fluid is found between the

    a. arachnoid mater and the dura mater.

    b. vertebrae and the meninges.

    c. pia mater and the arachnoid mater.

27. The spinal cord ends

    a. at the sacrum.

    b. between thoracic vertebrae 11 and 12.

    c. between lumbar vertebrae 1 and 2.

    d. at lumbar vertebra 5.

28. Which of the following statements is/are true about the white matter in the spinal cord?

    a. A cross section of the cord reveals a core of white matter surrounded by gray matter.

    b. The white matter is composed of myelinated nerve fibers and makes up nerve pathways called tracts.

    c. The white matter carries sensory stimuli to the brain; the gray matter carries motor stimuli to the periphery.

    d. The nerve fibers within spinal tracts arise from cell bodies located in the same part of the nervous system.

29. The three major portions of the brain are the _____, _____, and _____.

30. The hemispheres of the cerebrum are connected by nerve fibers called the

    a. corpus callosum.

    b. falx cerebri.

    c. tissue of Rolando.

    d. tentorium.

31. Match the functions in the first column with the appropriate area of the brain in the second column.

     _____a. hearing   1.   frontal lobes

     _____b. vision   2.   parietal lobes

     _____c. recognition of printed work   3.   temporal lobes

     _____d. control of voluntary muscles   4.   occipital lobes

     _____e. pain

     _____f. complex problem solving

32. Which hemisphere of the brain is dominant for most of the population?

33. Cerebrospinal fluid is produced by the _____ _____.

34. The thalamus and hypothalamus are parts of the brain located in the

    a.   midbrain.   c.   medulla oblongata.

    b.   pons.   d.   diencephalon.

35. The part of the brain responsible for regulation of temperature and heart rate, control of hunger, and regulation of fluid and electrolytes is the

    a.   thalamus.   c.   medulla oblongata.

    b.   hypothalamus.   d.   pons.

36. The _____ _____ produces emotional reactions of fear, anger, and pleasure.

37. Consciousness is dependent on stimulation of the _____ _____.

38. Tremors, loss of muscle tone, gait disturbance, and a loss of equilibrium may be due to damage to the _____.

39. The peripheral nervous system has two divisions: the _____ nervous system and the _____ nervous system.

40. There are _____ pairs of cranial nerves; all but one of these arise from the _____ _____.

41. Vision and function of the eyes and associated structures are controlled by cranial nerves _____ through _____.

42. There are _____ pairs of spinal nerves.

43. The part of the nervous system that functions without conscious control is the _____ nervous system.

44. Nerves of the sympathetic division leave the spinal cord with spinal nerves in the _____ and _____.

45. Which of the following are responses to stimulation by the sympathetic nervous system?

    a.   increased heart rate   c.   increased peristalsis

    b.   increased blood glucose concentration   d.   increased salivation

46. Which of the following are responses to stimulation of the parasympathetic nervous system?

    a.   dilation of the bronchioles   c.   contraction of the gallbladder

    b.   dilation of the coronary arteries   d.   contraction of the muscles of the urinary bladder

STUDY ACTIVITIES

I.   Aids to Understanding Words

Define the following word parts. (p. 203)

ax-	moto-
dendr-	peri-
funi-	plex-
gangli-	sens-
-lemm	syn-
mening-	ventr-

II.   9.1 Introduction (p. 203)

A.   The structural and functional units of the nervous system are the _____.

B.   Neurons typically have many _____ and one _____.

C.   List the organs of the central and peripheral nervous systems.

D.   What does the nervous system allow us to do?

III.   9.2 General Functions of the Nervous System (pp. 204–205)

A.   Describe the general functions of the nervous system.

sensory

integrative

motor

B.   Describe the somatic and autonomic nervous systems.

IV. 9.3 Neuroglial Cells (pp. 205–206)

A. Label the following structures in the accompanying illustration: ependymal cell, ashocyte, neurons, oligodendrocyte microglial cells, capillary axon, myelin sheath (cut), node.

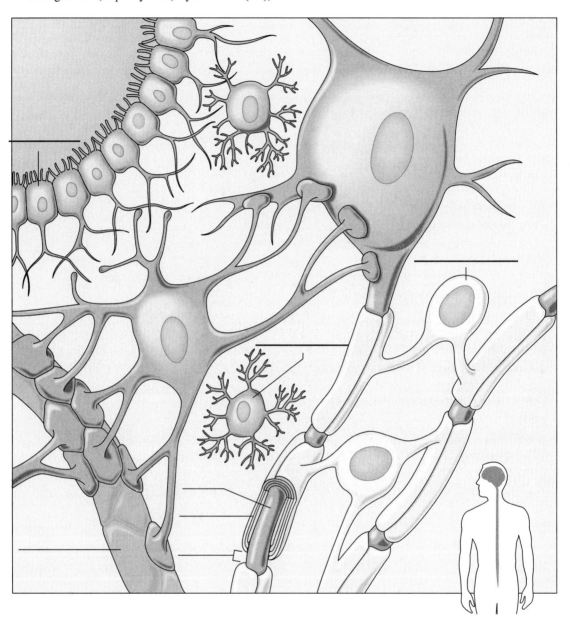

B. Fill in the following chart comparing supporting cells of the nervous system.

Neuroglial Cells	Location	Function
Microglial cells		
Oligodendrocytes		
Astrocytes		
Ependymal cells		
Schwann cells		

A. Label the following structures of a motor neuron shown in the accompanying illustration: dendrites, axon, nucleolus, cell body, nucleus, neurofibrils, nodes of Ranvier, myelin, nucleus of Schwann cell, axonal hillock, chromatophilic substance, synaptic knob of axon terminal, portion of a collateral.

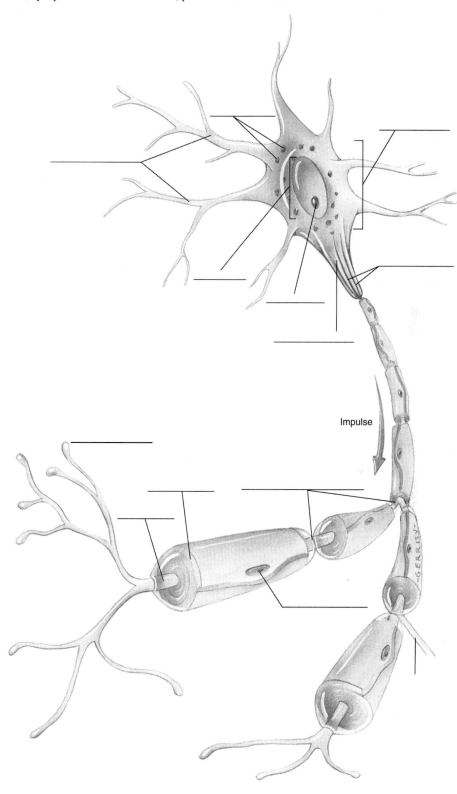

Impulse

B.   Answer these questions about neuron structure.

    1. List the basic structures common to all neurons.

    2. List and describe the organelles of the neuron cell body.

    3. The main receptive structures of neurons are _____. Describe them briefly.

    4. Describe how Schwann cells make up the myelin sheath and the neurolemma on the outsides of nerve fibers.

    5. Narrow gaps in the myelin sheath between the Schwann cells are the _____ _____ _____.

C.   Neurons can be classified by structure. Describe and locate these neurons. (pp. 218–219)

    bipolar neurons

    unipolar neurons

    multipolar neurons

D.   Neurons can also be classified by function. Fill in the following table. (pp. 208–209)

Location and function of neurons classified by function

Neuron	Location	Function
Sensory neurons		
Interneurons		
Motor neurons		

VI.   9.5 Cell Membrane Potential (pp. 210–213)

A.   The outside of a cell membrane is usually electrically charged with respect to the inside, due to a(n) _____ distribution of _____ _____ _____ _____ on either side of the membrane. (p. 212)

B.   Describe the events occurring in the cell membrane that permit conduction of an impulse. (p. 213)

C.   Describe membrane polarization, depolarization, and repolarization. Which of these events is a nerve impulse? (pp. 213–214)

A.   How do the nodes of Ranvier affect nerve impulse conduction? What kind of conduction is this called? (p. 216)

B.   Define the all-or-none response in neurons. (pp. 213–214)

C.   What is the refractory period?

VIII.   9.7 The Synapse (pp. 214–216)

A.   Answer these questions concerning synaptic transmission. (p. 215)

     1.   Label the following structures in the accompanying drawing of a synapse: synaptic vesicles, synaptic cleft, neurotransmitter, polarized membrane, axon membrane, synaptic knob, depolarized membrane, vesicle-releasing neurotransmitter, dendrite of post synaptic neuron.

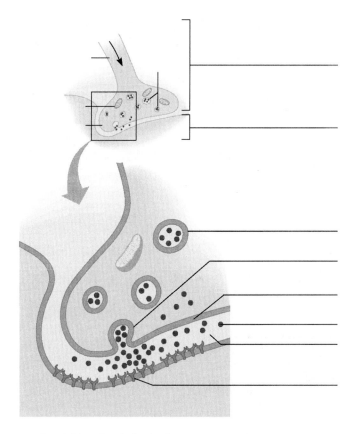

     2.   How does a neurotransmitter initiate depolarization?

     3.   List substances that function as neurotransmitters.

B.   Answer these questions concerning excitatory and inhibitory actions. (p. 214)

    1.   Describe excitatory and inhibitory actions. How do they interact in normal nerve function?

    2.   What substances seem to have inhibitory action?

    3.   How is stimulation of the nerve fiber stopped?

IX.   9.8 Impulse Processing (pp. 216–217)

A.   Describe the role of neuronal pools in producing facilitation, convergence, and divergence. (pp. 216–217)

B.   What is Facilitation?

C.   What is Convergence?

D.   What is Divergence?

X.   9.9 Types of Nerves (pp. 217–218)

A.   What is a nerve?

B.   What is a motor nerve?

C.   What is a sensory nerve?

D.   What is a mixed nerve?

XI. 9.10 Nerve Pathways (pp. 218–220)

A. What is a nerve pathway? (p. 218)

B. What is a reflex? What is a reflex arc? (p. 218)

C. Label the following parts of the reflex shown in the drawing: dendrite of sensory neuron, cell body of sensory neuron, axon of sensory neuron, dendrite of motor neuron, cell body of motor neuron, axon of motor neuron, spinal cord, receptor ends of sensory neuron, effector-quadriceps femoris muscle group, patella, patellar ligament. (p. 219)

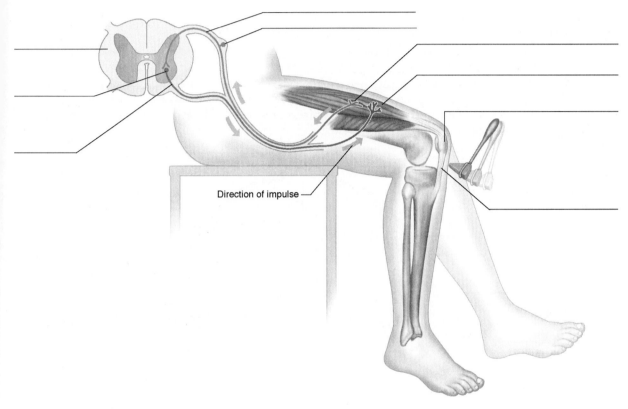

Direction of impulse

XII. 9.11 Meninges (pp. 220–221)

A. What are the bony coverings of the central nervous system? (p. 220)

B.   Fill in the following table. (p. 220)

The meninges

Layer	Location	Structure and special features	Function
Dura mater			
Arachnoid mater			
Pia mater			

XIII. 9.12 Spinal Cord (pp. 221–224)

A.   Answer these questions concerning the structure of the spinal cord. (pp. 221–222)

    1. The superior boundary of the spinal cord is _____. The inferior boundary of the spinal cord is _____.

    2. Label the accompanying drawing of a cross section of the spinal cord: anterior median fissure, posterior median sulcus, white matter, gray matter, posterior horn, lateral horn, anterior horn, gray commissure, central canal, lateral funiculus, dorsal root of spinal nerve, dorsal root ganglion, ventral root of spinal nerve, spinal nerve, anterior funiculus, posterior funiculus.

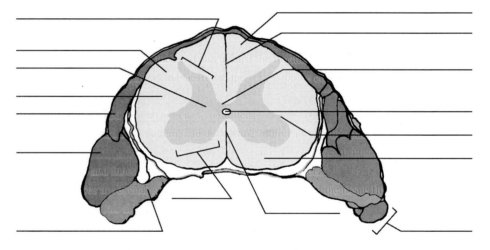

    3. There are _____ pair of spinal nerves.

B.   What is the effect of injury to ascending tracts? To descending tracts? (pp. 222–223)

C.   Define *pyramidal* and *extrapyramidal tracts*. (p. 223)

XIV. 9.13 Brain (pp. 224–233)

A.   List the parts of the brain. (pp. 224–225)

B.   Answer these questions concerning the structure of the cerebrum. (pp. 225–226)

    1. The bridge that connects the two hemispheres is the _____ _____.

    2. The ridges of the hemispheres are _____.

3.   A shallow groove is a(n) _____ ; a deeper groove is a(n) _____ .

4.   Name the lobes of the cerebral hemispheres.

5.   The outer layer of the cerebrum is the _____ . It is composed of _____

_____ .

6.   The inner layer of the cerebrum is composed of _____ _____ .

C.   Answer these questions concerning the function of the cerebrum. (pp. 226–227)

1.   What are the functions of the cerebrum?

2.   Fill in the following table.

Functional areas of the cerebrum

Areas	Locations	Function
Motor		
Sensory		
Association		

D.   Describe the functions of the dominant and nondominant hemispheres of the brain. (p. 227)

E.   List the basal ganglia.

F.   Answer these questions concerning the ventricles and cerebrospinal fluid. (pp. 227–228)

1.   Describe the location of the four ventricles.

2.   Where is cerebrospinal fluid secreted? What is its function?

G.   Answer these questions concerning the diencephalon. (p. 229)

1.   Locate the diencephalon and describe its structure.

2.   Fill in the following table.

Functions of the diencephalon

Structure	Location	Function
Thalamus		
Hypothalamus		

3.   What structures comprise the limbic system? What is the function of this system? (p. 230)

H.   Answer these questions concerning the brain stem. (pp. 230–232)
    1.   Where is the brain stem? What are its component structures?

    2.   Where is the midbrain located? What is its function?

    3.   Where is the pons located? What is its function?

    4.   Where is the medulla oblongata located? The medulla is the control center for what vital activities?

    5.   Describe the location, structure, and function of the reticular formation.

I.   What is the function of the cerebellum? (pp. 232–233)

XV. 9.14 Peripheral Nervous System (pp. 233–237)

A.   Answer these questions concerning the parts of the peripheral nervous system. (p. 233)
    1.   What are the parts of the peripheral nervous system?

    2.   What is the function of the somatic nervous system? The autonomic nervous system?

B.   Answer these questions concerning the cranial nerves. (pp. 233–235)
    1.   An easy way to memorize the names of the cranial nerves is to use the following sentence.

         On old Olympus towering tops a Finn and German viewed some hops.
         I II III   IV   V VI VII VIII IX   X   XI XII

         (Remember that VIII can be called auditory, and XI can be called spinal accessory.)

2. You need to be able to identify the cranial nerves by both name and number. Fill in the following table.

Cranial nerve functions

Cranial nerve		Sensory, motor, or mixed	Function
I	Olfactory		
II	Optic		
III	Oculomotor		
IV	Trochlear		
V	Trigeminal		
VI	Abducens		
VII	Facial		
VIII	Vestibulocochlear or Auditory		
IX	Glossopharyngeal		
X	Vagus		
XI	Accessory or Spinal Accessory		
XII	Hypoglossal		

C. Answer these questions concerning spinal nerves. (pp. 236–237)

1. How are the spinal nerves identified?

2. What is the structure and function of the dorsal root? Of the ventral root?

D. Answer these questions concerning spinal nerve plexuses. (p. 237)

1. What is a plexus?

2. Fill in the following table.

Spinal nerve plexuses

Plexus	Nerves involved	Structures innervated
Cervical plexuses		
Brachial plexuses		
Lumbosacral plexuses		

XVI. **9.15 Autonomic Nervous System (pp. 237–242)**

A. Describe the characteristics of the autonomic nervous system. (pp. 237–238)

B. The divisions of the autonomic nervous system are the _____ and the _____ divisions. (p. 238).

C. How are the nerve pathways of the autonomic division different from those of the somatic division? (pp. 238–240)

D. Where do the preganglionic fibers originate in each division? (pp. 238–240)

E. Identify the neurotransmitters associated with pre- and post-ganglionic fibers in the sympathetic and parasympathetic divisions. (p. 240)

XVII.   Clinical Focus Question

Multiple sclerosis is a disease in which myelin is destroyed, leading to the formation of plaques or scars in the central nervous system. The course of the disease is characterized by periods of remission and exacerbation.

1.   How might nerve transmission be affected?

2.   Remission may be due to replacement of myelin. Which of the glial cells would be involved in this process?

3.   The symptoms of multiple sclerosis depend on the location and duration of the characteristic lesions. Predict the expected symptoms if the lesion is located in the following areas:

optic nerves

brain stem

cerebellum

corticospinal tracts

white matter of the cerebral cortex

When you have finished the study activities to your satisfaction, retake the mastery test and compare your results with your initial attempt. If you are not satisfied with your performance, repeat the appropriate study activities.

CHAPTER **10**
SOMATIC AND SPECIAL SENSES

OVERVIEW

This chapter deals with specialized parts of the nervous system that allow the body to assess and adjust to the external environment. It describes the locations and structures of the somatic and special senses, and the function of each in maintaining homeostasis (objectives 1–14).

An understanding of these senses is necessary to know how the nervous system receives input and responds to support life.

CHAPTER OBJECTIVES

After you have studied this chapter, you should be able to:

10.1   Introduction
     1. Distinguish between somatic senses and special senses.

10.2   Receptors and Sensations
     2. Name five kinds of receptors and explain their functions.
     3. Explain how a sensation arises.

10.3   Somatic Senses
     4. Describe the receptors associated with the senses of touch, pressure, temperature, and pain.
     5. Describe how the sense of pain is produced.

10.4   Special Senses

10.5   Sense of Smell
     6. Identify the location of the receptors associated with the special senses.
     7. Explain the relationship between the senses of smell and taste.
     8. Explain the hypothesized mechanism for smell.

10.6   Sense of Taste
     9. Explain the mechanism for taste.

10.7   Sense of Hearing
     10. Name the parts of the ear, and explain the function of each part.

10.8   Sense of Equilibrium
     11. Distinguish between static and dynamic equilibrium.

10.9   Sense of Sight
     12. Name the parts of the eye, and explain the function of each part.
     13. Explain how the eye refracts light.
     14. Describe the visual nerve pathway.

FOCUS QUESTION

When you began this chapter at 3:00 P.M., it was 32° F outside, but the sun was pouring into the room. It is now after 5:00 P.M., and as you reach to turn on the light, you notice the room has become chilly, so you get a sweater. You smell the supper your roommate is preparing, and you realize you are hungry. How have your special senses functioned to process and act on this sensory information?

MASTERY TEST

Now take the mastery test. Do not guess. As soon as you complete the test, correct it. Note your successes and failures so that you can read the chapter to meet your learning needs.

1.   List 5 kinds of receptors and what stimulates them.

2.   Perception of sensory impulses results from
    a.   the type of receptor stimulated   c.   the region of the brain that receives the impulse
    b.   the nature of impulse conduction   d.   prior experience with the type of impulse

3.   List the location for receptors associated with the somatic senses.

4.   Meissner's corpuscles and Pacinian corpuscles are sensitive to
    a.   touch and pressure.   c.   heat.
    b.   pain.   d.   light.

5.   Sensory receptors for all of the following adapt to repeated stimulation by sending fewer and fewer impulses, *except* those for
    a.   heat.   c.   pain.
    b.   light.   d.   touch.

6.   Pain receptors respond to the release of _____.

7.   Which of the following events will elicit pain from visceral organs?
    a.   spasm of smooth muscle   c.   stretching of a visceral organ
    b.   cutting into the viscera   d.   burning, as in electrocautery

8.   Sharp pain that disappears when the pain stimulus is stopped is _____pain.

9.   In what area of the brain do pain fibers terminate?

10.   Pain-suppressing substances found in the pituitary gland and the hypothalamus are _____.

11.   List the special senses.

12.   The receptors for taste and smell are examples of
    a.   mechanical receptors.   c.   thermoreceptors.
    b.   chemoreceptors.

13.   Olfactory receptors are located in the
    a.   nasopharynx.   c.   superior nasal conchae.
    b.   inferior nasal conchae.   d.   lateral wall of the nostril.

14.   Impulses that stimulate the olfactory receptors are transmitted along the _____ _____.

15.   The sensitive part of a taste bud is the
    a.   taste cell.   c.   taste hair.
    b.   taste pore.

16.   Saliva enhances the taste of food by
    a.   increasing the motility of taste receptors.   c.   releasing taste factors by partially digesting
    b.   dissolving the chemicals that cause taste.   food.

17.   The four primary taste sensations are _____, _____, _____, and _____.

18.   In addition to the sense of hearing, the ear also functions in the sense of _____.

19.   The functions of the small bones of the middle ear are to
    a.   provide a framework for the tympanic membrane.   c.   transmit vibrations from the external ear to the inner ear.
    b.   protect the structures of the inner ear.   d.   increase the force of vibrations transmitted to the inner ear.

20.   A means of providing equal pressure on both sides of the eardrum is furnished by the _____ _____.

21. The inner ear consists of two complex structures called the _____ _____ and the _____ .

22. Hearing receptors are located in the
   a. organ of Corti.
   b. scala vestibuli.
   c. scala tympani.
   d. round window.

23. The hair cells of the vestibule are stimulated by
   a. bending the head forward or backward.
   b. rapid turns of the head or body.
   c. changes in the position of the body relative to the ground.
   d. changes in the position of skeletal muscles.

24. The organ(s) of dynamic equilibrium are the _____ _____ .

25. The muscle that raises the eyelid is the
   a. orbicularis oculi.
   b. superior rectus.
   c. levator palpebrae superioris.
   d. ciliary muscle.

26. The conjunctiva covers the anterior surface of the eyeball, except for the _____ .

27. The superior rectus muscle rotates the eye
   a. upward and toward the midline.
   b. toward the midline.
   c. away from the midline.
   d. upward and away from the midline.

28. The transparency of the cornea is due to the
   a. nature of the cytoplasm in the cells of the cornea.
   b. small number of cells and the lack of blood vessels.
   c. lack of nuclei within these cells.
   d. keratinization of cells in the cornea.

29. In the posterior wall of the eyeball, the sclera is pierced by the _____ _____ .

30. The shape of the lens changes as the eye focuses on a close object in a process known as
   a. accommodation.
   b. refraction.
   c. reflection.
   d. strabismus.

31. The anterior chamber of the eye extends from the _____ to the iris.

32. The part of the eye that controls the amount of light entering the eye is the _____ .

33. The inner tunic of the eye contains the receptor cells of sight and is called the _____ .

34. The region associated with the sharpest vision is the
   a. macula lutea.
   b. fovea centralis.
   c. optic disk.
   d. choroid coat.

35. The bending of light waves as they pass at an oblique angle from a medium of one optical density to a medium of another optical density is called _____ .

36. There are two types of visual receptors: one is called_____ , and the other is called _____ .

37. Match the type of vision in the first column with the proper receptor from the second column.
   _____a. vision in relatively dim light
   _____b. color vision
   _____c. general outlines
   _____d. sharp images
   1. rods
   2. cones

38. The light-sensitive pigment in rods is _____ . In the presence of light, this pigment decomposes to form _____ and _____ .

39. Some of the fibers of the optic nerves cross within the _____ _____ .

STUDY ACTIVITIES

1. Aids to Understanding Words

Define the following words and word parts. (p. 249)

choroid	olfact-
cochlea	scler-
iris	tympan-
labyrinth	vitre-
lacri-	
macula	

II.   10.1 Introduction (p. 249)

A.   What is the function of sensory receptors? (p. 249)

B.   List the somatic senses and the special senses. How are they different?

III.   10.2 Receptors and Sensations (p. 249)

A.   List five groups of sensory receptors.

B.   The process that allows an individual to locate the region of stimulation is called _____.

C.   The process that makes a receptor ignore a continuous stimulus unless the strength of that stimulus is increased is _____ _____.

D.   What is a sensation?

IV.   10.3 Somatic Senses (pp. 249–253)

A.   Fill in the following table. (pp. 249–250)

Cutaneous receptors

Type	Structure/Location	Sensation
Sensory nerve fibers (mechanoreceptors)		
Meissner's corpuscles (mechanoreceptors)		
Pacinian corpuscles		
Temperature senses		
Free nerve endings (pain receptors)		

B.	Answer these questions concerning pain receptors. (pp. 250–253)

    1.	How do pain receptors differ from the other somatic senses?

    2.	What events trigger visceral pain?

    3.	What is referred pain?

    4.	Compare acute pain fibers and chronic pain fibers.

    5.	How does the brain regulate pain impulses?

## V.	10.4 Special Senses (p. 253)

List the special senses.

## VI.	10.5 Sense of Smell (pp. 253–255)

A.	The sense of smell supplements the sense of _____. (p. 253)

B.	On the accompanying illustrations, label the olfactory tract, olfactory bulb, cribriform plate, nasal cavity, olfactory area of the nasal cavity, the superior nasal concha, nerve fibers within olfactory bulb, cilia, olfactory receptor cells, and columnar epithelial cells.

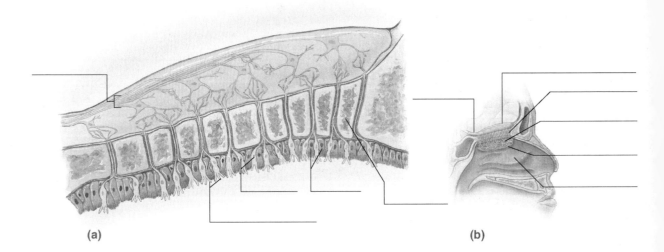

(a)	(b)

C.	How do odors stimulate olfactory receptors? (pp. 254–255)

VII.   **10.6 Sense of Taste (pp. 255–256)**

A.   Describe the structure of taste receptors. (p. 255)

B.   How does saliva contribute to the perception of taste? (p. 256)

C.   Label the following structures in the accompanying illustration of taste buds: epithelium of the tongue, taste cell, taste hair, supporting cell, taste pore, sensory nerve fibers, connective tissue.

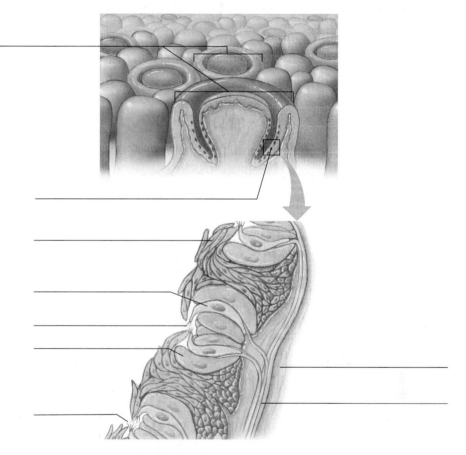

D.   1.   List four primary taste sensations.

      2.   What areas of the tongue are associated with each taste?

E.   Describe the nerve pathways for taste. (p.256)

VIII.   10.7 Sense of Hearing (pp. 256–261)

A.   Describe the function of the external ear. (p. 256)

B.   Describe the vibration-conduction pathway of the ear from the meatus to the temporal lobe of the cerebrum. (pp. 257–258)

C.   Why does it help to chew gum while descending in an airplane? (pp. 257–258)

D.   Describe the function of the inner ear. (pp. 258–260)

E.   Contrast conductive and sensorineural deafness. (p. 261)

F.   Describe the nerve pathways for hearing. (pp. 260–261)

IX.   10.8 Sense of Equilibrium (pp. 261–262)

A.   Distinguish between static and dynamic equilibrium.

B.   Describe the function of each of the following structures in maintaining equilibrium.

   Utricle   crista ampullaris

   Saccule   cerebellum

   Macula   eyes

   semicircular canals

X.   10.9 Sense of Sight (pp. 262–272)

A.   Answer these questions concerning the visual accessory organs. (pp. 262–265)
   1.   What structures are covered by the conjunctiva?

   2.   Describe the lacrimal apparatus. How does it protect the eye?

3. Identify the function of the following muscles.

orbicularis oculi   medial rectus

levator palpebrae superioris   lateral rectus

superior rectus   superior oblique

inferior rectus   inferior oblique

B. Label the following structures in the accompanying illustration: cornea, lens, iris, suspensory ligaments, vitreous humor, aqueous humor, sclera, optic disk, optic nerve, fovea centralis, retina, choroid coat, pupil, ciliary body, anterior cavity, posterior cavity, anterior chamber, posterior chamber, lateral rectus, and medial rectus. What is the function of each of the labeled structures? (p. 266)

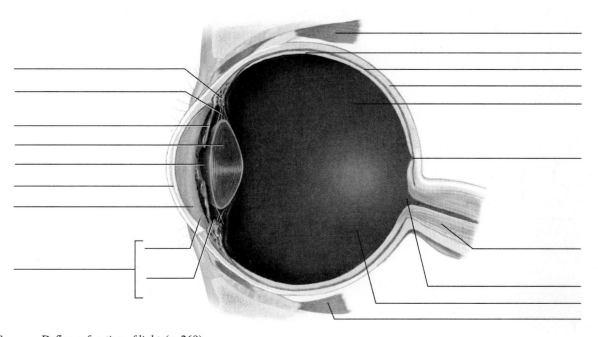

C. Define *refraction of light.* (p. 269)

D. Answer these questions concerning visual receptors. (p. 270)
   1. Describe the functions of rods.

   2. Describe the location and functions of cones.

   3. What mechanism is used by cones to recognize color?

E. Describe the visual nerve pathway. (pp. 271–272)

XI. Clinical Focus Question

A.   Compare the loss of vision due to cataracts and glaucoma. How are each of these conditions treated?

B.   What are the symptoms of cataracts? Of glaucoma?

C.   How are each of these vision problems treated?

D.   How many cranial nerves are devoted to the sense of sight?

E.   What conclusions can be drawn based on your response?

When you have finished the study activities to your satisfaction, retake the mastery test and compare your results with your initial attempt. If you are not satisfied with your performance, repeat the appropriate study activities.

## CHAPTER 11

ENDOCRINE SYSTEM

OVERVIEW

The endocrine system, like the nervous system, controls body activities to maintain a relatively constant internal environment. The methods used by these two systems are different. This chapter describes the difference between endocrine and exocrine glands, the location of the endocrine glands, and the hormones they secrete (objectives 1–5). It explains the nature of hormones, the substances that function as hormones, how hormones affect target tissues, how the secretion of hormones is controlled by a negative feedback system and the nervous system, the general function of each hormone, and the result of too little or too much of each hormone (objectives 6–12). Mediation of stress is also discussed (objective 13).

A knowledge of the function of the endocrine system is basic to understanding how metabolic processes are regulated to meet the changing needs of the body.

CHAPTER OBJECTIVES

After you have studied this chapter, you should be able to:

11.1   Introduction
   1. Define hormone.
   2. Distinguish between poracrine and autocrine glands.
   3. Distinguish between endocrine and exocrine glands.

11.2   General Characteristics of the Endocrine System
   4. Explain how the neurons and endocrine systems are alike and how they differ.
   5. Describe the source of specificity of the endocrine system.
   6. Name some functions of hormones.

11.3   Hormone Action
   7. Explain how steroid and nonsteroid hormones affect target cells.

11.4   Control of Hormone Secretions
   8. Discuss how negative feedback mechanisms regulate hormonal secretions.
   9. Explain how the nervous system controls hormonal secretion.

11.5–11.10   Pituitary Gland—Other Endocrine Glands
   10. Name and describe the location of the major endocrine glands, and list the hormones they secrete.
   11. Describe the general functions of the hormones that endocrine glands secrete.
   12. Explain how the secretion of each hormone is regulated.

11.11   Stress and Health
   13. Define stress, and describe how the body responds to it.

FOCUS QUESTION

How does the endocrine system complement the nervous system in maintaining a person's ability to interact with both external and internal environments?

MASTERY TEST

Now take the mastery test. Do not guess. As soon as you complete the test, correct it. Note your successes and failures so that you can read the chapter to meet your learning needs.

1. Chemical signals sent between individuals are _____.

2. A chemical messenger involved in the regulation of body functions is a _____.

3. Local hormones are secreted by _____ and _____ glands.

4. Glands that secrete substances to the outside of the body are _____ glands.

5. Glands that release their secretions directly into the body fluids and help regulate metabolic processes are _____ glands.

6. Many hormones are thought to function by acting on receptor sites in the

    a. target cells.   c. genes.
    b. nucleus.   d. cytoplasm.

7. A major difference between steroid and nonsteroid hormones is the degree to which they

    a. can be manufactured as drugs.   c. can be excreted by the kidney.
    b. are lipid soluble.   d. require metabolism in the liver.

8. Another group of compounds that have hormonelike effects are _____.

9. The characteristics of the negative feedback system that regulate hormone secretion include

    a. activation by imbalance.   c. exertion of a stimulating effect on the
                                                   gland.
    b. exertion of an inhibitory effect on the gland.   d. a tendency for levels of hormone to fluctuate.

10. The part of the brain most closely related to endocrine function is the _____.

11. The anterior and posterior lobes of the pituitary gland are regulated by the _____.

12. The hormones secreted by the anterior lobe of the pituitary gland include

    a. thyroid-stimulating hormones.   c. antidiuretic hormone.
    b. luteinizing hormone.   d. oxytocin.

13. Which of the following are actions of pituitary growth hormone?

    a. enhance the movement of amino acids through   c. increase the utilization of fats by cells
        the cell membrane   d. enhance the movement of potassium across
    b. increase the utilization of glucose by cells   the cell membrane

14. The pituitary hormone that stimulates and maintains milk production following childbirth is _____.

15. TSH secretion is regulated by

    a. circulating thyroid hormones.   c. osmolarity of blood.
    b. blood sugar levels.   d. TRH secreted by the hypothalamus.

16. Which of the following pituitary hormones regulate(s) fluid balance?

    a. LSH   c. FSH
    b. ADH   d. oxytocin

17. A hormone of the posterior pituitary gland plays a major role in regulating the amount of water in the body.

    a. true
    b. false

18. The thyroid hormones that affect the metabolic rate are _____ and _____.

19. Which of the following are functions of thyroid hormones?

    a. control sodium levels   c. increase protein synthesis
    b. decrease rate of energy release from   d. accelerate growth in children
        carbohydrates

20. The element necessary for normal function of the thyroid gland is _____.

21. The thyroid hormone that tends to keep calcium in the bone is _____.

22. Hypothyroidism in an infant is characterized by

    a.   hyperactivity.
                c.   excessive appetite.

    b.   mental retardation.
                d.   abnormal bone formation.

23. Which of the following statements about parathormone (parathyroid hormone) is(are) true?

    a.   Parathormone enhances absorption of calcium from the intestine.
                c.   Parathormone stimulates the kidneys to conserve calcium.

    b.   Parathormone stimulates the bone to release ionized calcium.
                d.   Parathormone secretion is stimulated by the hypothalamus.

24. Injury to or removal of parathyroid glands is likely to result in

    a.   reduced osteoclastic activity.
                c.   kidney stones.

    b.   Cushing's disease.
                d.   hypocalcemia.

25. The hormones of the adrenal medulla are _____ and _____.

26. The adrenal hormone aldosterone belongs to a category of cortical hormones called

    a.   mineralocorticoids.
                c.   sex hormones.

    b.   glucocorticoids.

27. The actions of cortisol include

    a.   the breakdown of stored protein to increase the levels of circulating amino acids.
                c.   stimulation of gluconeogenesis.

                                d.   conservation of water.

    b.   increased release of fatty acids and decreased use of glucose.

28. Adrenal sex hormones are primarily (male, female).

29. The endocrine portion of the pancreas are cells called _____ _____

_____.

30. The hormone that responds to a low blood sugar by stimulating the liver to convert glycogen to glucose is

_____.

31. The action of insulin that most directly leads to lowered blood sugar levels is

    a.   enhancing glucose absorption from the small intestine.
                c.   promoting the transport of amino acids out of the cell.

    b.   facilitating the transport of glucose across the cell membrane.
                d.   increasing the synthesis of fats.

32. The most common type of diabetes mellitus is (Type I, Type II).

33. The hormone melatonin is secreted by the

    a.   thymus.
                c.   gonads.

    b.   pineal gland.

34. A negative side effect of the general stress syndrome is increased susceptibility to _____.

35. Stressors may be positive or negative stimuli.

    a.   true

    b.   false

36. What gland activates the "fight or flight" mechanism?

    a.   hypothalamus
                c.   adrenal cortex

    b.   thalamus
                d.   adrenal medulla

STUDY ACTIVITIES

I. Aids to Understanding Words

Define the following word parts. (p. 277)

-crin   hyper-

diuret-   para-

endo-   toc-

exo-   hypo-

II. 11.1 Introduction and Clinical Example (pp. 276–277)

A.   Discuss the role of phenomes in the reproductive behavior of species, including insects, rodents, and humans. (p. 276)

B.   What is a hormone?

C.   List the differences between endocrine and exocrine glands. (p. 277)

D.   How do paracrine and autocrine glands differ from both endocrine and exocrine glands?

III. 11.2 General Characteristics of the Endocrine System (pp. 277–278)

A.   As a group, endocrine glands regulate _____ _____.

B.   List the ways in which endocrine glands accomplish their general function.

IV. 11.3 Hormone Action (pp. 278–281)

A.   The specific site of a hormone's action is called its _____ _____. (p. 277)

B.   Describe how hormones are synthesized.

C.   Compare the characteristics of steroid and nonsteroid hormones. (pp. 278–280)

D. What is the role of cyclic adenosine monophosphate? (p. 280)

E. What are prostaglandins? (p. 281)

V. 11.4 Control of Hormonal Secretions (pp. 281–282)

A. List the three mechanisms that control hormone secretion.

B. Describe how the negative feedback system regulates hormone secretion. (p. 282)

C. How does the nervous system control hormone secretion? (p. 282)

VI. 11.5 Pituitary Gland (pp. 282–286)

A. Describe the structure and location of the pituitary gland. (p. 282)

B.   Fill in the following table. (pp. 282–286)

Hormones of the pituitary gland

Hormone	Stimulus for secretion	Actions (be specific)
Anterior lobe		
Growth hormone		
Prolactin		
Thyroid-stimulating hormone		
Adrenocorticotropic hormone		
Follicle-stimulating hormone		
Luteinizing hormone		
Posterior lobe		
Antidiuretic hormone		
Oxytocin		

VII.   11.6 Thyroid Gland (pp. 286–288)

A.   In the accompanying illustration, label the thyroid gland, isthmus, larynx, colloid, follicular cell, and extrafollicular cell. (p. 301)

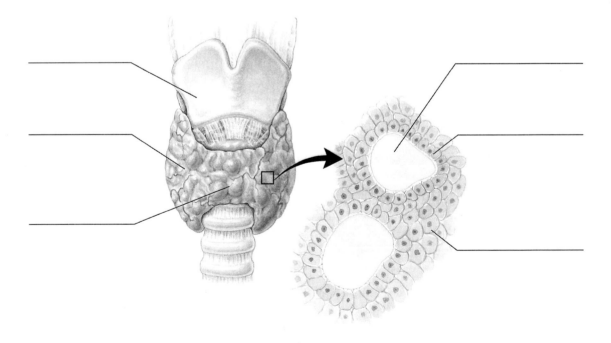

B.   Answer these questions concerning thyroid hormones and their functions. (pp. 289–291)
    1.   What element is needed to synthesize thyroxine and triiodothyronine?

    2.   What are the functions of thyroxine and triiodothyronine?

VIII.   11.7 Parathyroid Glands (p. 288)

A.   Where are the parathyroid glands located?

B.   Describe how parathyroid hormone affects blood levels of calcium and phosphorus. Include its effect on bone, the intestine, and the kidneys.

C.   What is the function of calcitonin?

IX.   11.8 Adrenal Glands (pp. 288–292)

A.   Where are the adrenal glands located? (p. 288)

B.   Answer these questions concerning hormones of the adrenal medulla. (p. 290)
    1.   List the hormones secreted by the adrenal medulla.

    2.   What are the effects of these hormones?

C.   Fill in the following table. (pp. 290–292)

Adrenocortical hormones

	Zone of the cortex	Stimulus for secretion	Effects of hormone
Mineralocorticoids (e.g., aldosterone)			
Glucocorticoids (e.g., cortisol)			
Sex hormones			

D.   Describe the negative feedback mechanism that controls the release of cortisol. (p. 291)

X.   11.9 Pancreas (pp. 292–294)

A.   Where is the pancreas located? (p. 292)

B.   Fill in the following table. (p. 294)

Hormones of the pancreas

	Source of control	Effects of hormone
Glucagon		
Insulin		

XI.   11.10 Other Endocrine Glands (pp. 294–295)

A.   Where is the pineal gland located, and what is its function? (p. 295)

B.   Where is the thymus gland located, and what is its function? (p. 295)

XII.   11.11 Stress and Health (p. 296)

A.   List examples of events that the body may respond to as stressors.

B.   Describe the general stress syndrome.

C.   What are the positive effects of the stress syndrome?

D.   What are the negative effects of the stress syndrome?

XIII. Clinical Focus Question

How do food intake, exercise, and insulin interact to control levels of glucose in the blood? How does stress affect this process?

When you have finished the study activities to your satisfaction, retake the mastery test and compare your results with your initial attempt. If you are not satisfied with your performance, repeat the appropriate study activities.

OVERVIEW

This chapter deals with a major connective tissue—the blood. It describes the general characteristics and major functions of blood (objective 1) and identifies the various types of blood cells, and the components and functions of plasma (objectives 2, 4, 6). It also explains blood typing, control of red blood cell production, blood coagulation, and reaction to mixing of blood types (objectives 3, 5, 6, 7, 8, 9).

Knowledge of the circulatory system expands the concept of how cells meet their need for oxygen. This knowledge also helps in understanding how the body recognizes and rejects foreign protein.

CHAPTER OBJECTIVES

After you have studied this chapter, you should be able to:

12.1   Introduction
   1.   Describe the general characteristics of blood and discuss its major functions.
12.2   Blood and Blood Cells
   2.   Distinguish among the formed elements of the blood.
   3.   Explain the control of red blood cell production.
   4.   Distinguish among the five types of white blood cells, and give the function(s) of each type.
12.3   Blood Plasma
   5.   List the major components of blood plasma, and describe the functions of each.
12.4   Hemostasis
   6.   Define *hemostasis,* and explain the mechanisms that help to achieve it.
   7.   Review the major steps in blood coagulation.
12.5   Blood Groups and Transfusions
   8.   Explain blood typing and how it is used to avoid adverse reactions following blood transfusions.
   9.   Describe how blood reactions may occur between fetal and maternal tissues.

FOCUS QUESTION

How does the structure of the blood help meet oxygenation needs, allow recognition and rejection of foreign protein, and control coagulation of the blood?

MASTERY TEST

Now take the mastery test. Do not guess. As soon as you complete the test, correct it. Note your successes and failures so that you can read the chapter to meet your learning needs.

1.   Blood is considered a type of _____ tissue.
2.   Plasma represents _____ percent of a normal blood sample.

3.	Which of the following formed elements of blood are essential to gas exchange?

    a.	platelets
                c.	white blood cells

    b.	red blood cells

4.	Which of the following statements is/are true?

    a.	Red blood cells have no nucleus.
                c.	The lack of a nucleus makes it easier for red blood cells to change their shape.

    b.	Red blood cells lose their nuclei to make more room for hemoglobin.
                d.	Red blood cells have a limited life span because they cannot synthesize protein.

5.	Red blood cell production is stimulated by the hormone _____, which is released from the kidney in response to low oxygen concentration.

6.	The average life span of a red blood cell is _____ _____.

7.	After birth, red blood cells are produced in

    a.	the spleen.
                c.	yellow marrow.

    b.	red marrow.
                d.	the liver.

8.	Does statement *a* explain statement *b*?_____

    a.	Vitamin B$_{12}$ and folic acid are necessary to cell growth and reproduction.

    b.	The rate of red blood cell reproduction makes this process especially dependent on vitamin B$_{12}$ and folic acid.

9.	The heme portion of damaged red blood cells is decomposed into iron and

    a.	biliverdin.
                c.	bile.

    b.	bilirubin.
                d.	granulocytes.

10.	Damaged red blood cells are destroyed by reticuloendothelial cells called

    a.	leukocytes.
                c.	neutrophils.

    b.	macrophages.
                d.	granulocytes.

11.	The cytokines that stimulate white blood cell production are _____ and _____ _____ _____.

12.	The most numerous type of white blood cell is the

    a.	neutrophil.
                c.	monocyte.

    b.	eosinophil.
                d.	lymphocyte.

13.	The white blood cell that forms antibodies necessary for immunity to specific diseases is the

    a.	basophil.
                c.	thrombocyte.

    b.	lymphocyte.
                d.	eosinophil.

14.	The normal white blood cell count is _____ to _____ per cubic millimeter (mm^3) of blood.

15.	White blood cells combat infection by

    a.	phagocytosis.
                c.	production of antibodies.

    b.	pinocytosis.
                d.	production of enzymes.

16.	The substances found in the cytoplasmic granules of basophils include _____ and _____.

17.	The blood element responsible for formation of clots and control of bleeding is the _____.

18.	Match the functions and characteristics in the first column with the appropriate plasma proteins from the second column.

    _____a.	largest molecular size
                1.	albumins

    _____b.	significant in maintaining osmotic pressure
                2.	globulins

    _____c.	transport(s) lipids and fat-soluble vitamins
                3.	fibrinogen

    _____d.	antibody(ies) of immunity

    _____e.	play(s) a part in blood clotting

19. The lipoproteins that have a relatively high concentration of cholesterol are
    a. chylomicrons.   c. low density lipoproteins.
    b. very low density lipoproteins.   d. high density lipoproteins.

20. The most abundant plasma electrolytes are
    a. calcium.   c. potassium.
    b. sodium.   d. chlorides.

21. A platelet plug begins to form when platelets are
    a. exposed to air.   c. exposed to calcium.
    b. exposed to a rough surface.   d. crushed.

22. The basic event in the formation of a blood clot is the transformation of a soluble plasma protein, _____, to a relatively insoluble protein, _____.

23. Substances believed necessary to activate prothrombin are thought to include
    a. calcium ions.   c. phospholipids.
    b. potassium ions.   d. glucose.

24. Prothrombin is a plasma protein that is produced by the
    a. kidney.   c. pancreas.
    b. small intestine.   d. liver.

25. Once a blood clot begins to form, it promotes still more clotting. This is an example of a(n)_____ _____ system.

26. A fragment of a blood clot that is traveling in the bloodstream is called a(n) _____.

27. The clumping together of red blood cells when unlike types of blood are mixed is due to antibodies in the plasma and antigens in the
    a. thrombocytes.   c. basophils.
    b. erythrocytes.   d. eosinophils.

28. A person with type A blood has
    a. agglutinogen A and agglutinin B.   c. agglutinins A and B.
    b. agglutinogens A and B.   d. neither agglutinin A nor B.

29. Agglutinins for Rh appear
    a. spontaneously as an inherited trait.   c. only in response to stimulation by Rh agglutinogens.
    b. only rarely for poorly understood reasons.

STUDY ACTIVITIES

I. Aids to Understanding Words

Define the following word parts. (p. 303)

agglutin-	leuko-
bil-	-osis
embol-	-poie
erythr-	-sta
Hem-	thromb-

II. 12.1 Introduction (p. 303)

What is the function of blood? (p. 303)

III.   **12.2 Blood and Blood Cells (pp. 303–310)**

A.   Answer these questions concerning the volume and composition of blood. (p. 303)
    1.   List the solid elements of the blood.

    2.   What is the blood volume of an average-sized (70 kg) male?

    3.   What part of blood tissue is plasma?

    4.   What are the components of plasma?

B.   Answer these questions concerning red blood cells. (p. 304)
    1.   The shape of a red blood cell is a(n) _____ _____.
    2.   How does the shape enhance the function of red blood cells?

    3.   Red blood cells are _____ red when carrying oxygen and are _____
          red when oxygen is released.
    4.   Why does the red blood cell lack a nucleus?

C.   Answer these questions concerning red blood cell counts. (p. 304)
    1.   What is the normal red blood cell count for a man? A woman?

    2.   What factors provoke a normal increase in red blood cells?

    3.   What dietary factors influence red blood cell production? (p. 305)

    4.   Where are red blood cells produced? (pp. 304–307)

    5.   How is the production of red blood cells controlled? (p. 305)

6.   How does sickle cell disease affect red blood cell production? (p. 305)

D.   Answer these questions concerning destruction of red blood cells. (pp. 305–307)
      1.   How are red blood cells damaged?

      2.   Damaged red blood cells are destroyed by cells called _____, located in the
            _____and _____.

E.   Fill in the following table. (pp. 307–310)

Types of white blood cells

White blood cell	Description	Percentage of total	Function
Granulocytes			
Neutrophil			
Eosinophil			
Basophil			
Agranulocytes			
Monocyte			
Lymphocyte			

F.   Answer these questions concerning white blood cell counts. (pp. 309–310)
      1.   What is a normal white cell count?

      2.   What causes an increase or a decrease in white blood cells?

3.   What is a differential white blood cell count?

G.   Describe the structure and function of platelets. (p. 310)

IV.   12.3 Blood Plasma (pp. 310–313)

A.   Fill in the following table. (pp. 310–312)

Plasma proteins

Protein	Description	Percent of total	Function
Albumins			
Globulins			
Fibrinogen			

B.   Answer these questions concerning nutrients and gases. (pp. 312–313)
    1.   What gases are found in plasma?

    2.   What nutrients are found in plasma?

    3.   Describe the nonprotein nitrogenous substances found in plasma.

C.   Answer these questions concerning plasma electrolytes. (p. 313)
    1.   What electrolytes are found in plasma?

    2.   What is the function of electrolytes?

V. 12.4 Hemostasis (pp. 314–316)

A.   List the mechanisms of hemostasis. (p. 314)

B.   How is a platelet plug formed? (p. 314)

C.   Describe the major events in the blood-clotting mechanism. (pp. 314–315)

D.   Describe the mechanisms that prevent coagulation. (p. 315)

E.   What is a thrombus? What is an embolus? What conditions predispose the formation of thrombi? (p. 315)

VI. 12.5 Blood Groups and Transfusions (pp. 316–320)

A.   Answer these questions concerning agglutinogens and agglutinins. (pp. 316–317)
1.   What are antigens (agglutinogens) and antibodies (agglutinins)?

2.   Antigens are present in the _____ _____; agglutinins are in the
_____.

B.   Answer these questions concerning the ABO blood group. (pp. 317–319)
1.   Describe the basis for ABO blood types.

2.   Why is it unsafe to mix different blood types?

C.   Answer these questions concerning the Rh blood group. (p. 319)
1.   What is the Rh factor?

2.   How does this differ from A, B, and O agglutinogens?

3. How does a fetus develop *erythroblastosis fetalis*?

VII. Clinical Focus Question

Fetal hemoglobin is constructed to maximize oxygen-carrying capacity in utero. This is important in understanding the development of symptoms of sickle cell disease.

1. Based on your knowledge of the life cycle of red blood cells, when do you expect the symptoms of sickle cell disease to appear?

2. What is the pathologic event that leads to sickle cell disease?

3. Why are children with sickle cell disease susceptible to infection?

4. What recommendations would you make to minimize the damage of sickle cell disease?

When you have finished the study activities to your satisfaction, retake the mastery test and compare your results with your initial attempt. If you are not satisfied with your performance, repeat the appropriate study activities.

CHAPTER 13
CARDIOVASCULAR SYSTEM

OVERVIEW

This chapter deals with the system that transports blood to and from cells—the cardiovascular system. It identifies the major organs of the cardiovascular system and explains their functions (objective 1). It discusses the location, structure, and function of the parts of the heart and the major types of blood vessels (objectives 2 and 6), and explains the pulmonary, systemic, and coronary circuits of the cardiovascular system and the major vessels in each circuit (objectives 3, 10, and 11). It discusses the cardiac cycle and its control, and relates these to the normal ECG (objectives 4 and 5). In addition, it describes how blood pressure is created and controlled, how venous blood is returned to the heart, and how substances are exchanged between capillary blood and tissue fluid (objectives 7–9).

After learning about the respiratory system and the blood, study of the cardiovascular system completes the knowledge of how oxygen is transported to cells and how waste products are transported away from cells.

CHAPTER OBJECTIVES

After you have studied this chapter, you should be able to:

13.1   Introduction
>   1. Name the organs of the cardiovascular system, and discuss their functions.

13.2   Structure of the Heart
>   2. Identify and locate the major parts of the heart and discuss the functions of each part.
>   3. Trace the pathway of the blood through the heart and the vessels of the coronary circulation.

13.3   Heart Actions
>   4. Discuss the cardiac cycle, and explain how it is controlled.
>   5. Identify the parts of a normal ECG pattern, and discuss the significance of this pattern.

13.4   Blood Vessels
>   6. Compare the structures and functions of the major types of blood vessels.
>   7. Describe how substances are exchanged between blood in capillaries and the tissue fluid surrounding body cells.
>   8. Describe the mechanisms that aid in returning venous blood to the heart.

13.5   Blood Pressure
>   9. Explain how blood pressure is produced and controlled.

13.6   Paths of Circulation
>   10. Compare the pulmonary and systemic circuits of the cardiovascular system.

13.7–13.8   Arterial System–Venous System
>   11. Identify and locate the major arteries and veins of the pulmonary and systemic circuits.

FOCUS QUESTION

How does the cardiovascular system work with the respiratory system to help your body remain in equilibrium when walking up the steps to your class and when sitting in class taking notes?

MASTERY TEST

Now take the mastery test. Do not guess. As soon as you complete the test, correct it. Note your successes and failures so that you can read the chapter to meet your learning needs.

1.   The heart is a cone-shaped, muscular pump located within the _____ _____.

2.   The base of the heart is located:
      a.   behind the second rib   c.   between the fourth and fifth rib
      b.   under the sternum
3.   The visceral pericardium is also known as the
      a.   epicardium.   c.   endocardium.
      b.   myocardium.
4.   Does statement *a* explain statement *b*?
      a.   Pericarditis is an inflammation of a membrane covering the heart.
      b.   Pericarditis destroys the contractile nature of the myocardium.
5.   Purkinje fibers are located in the
      a.   epicardium.   c.   endocardium.
      b.   myocardium.   d.   parietal pericardium.
6.   The upper chambers of the heart are the right and left _____; the lower chambers are the right and left _____.
7.   The vessels that empty into the upper right chamber of the heart are
      a.   inferior and superior venae cavae.   c.   pulmonary arteries.
      b.   pulmonary veins.   d.   coronary sinus.
8.   The valve between the chambers of the left side of the heart is the
      a.   semilunar valve.   c.   tricuspid valve.
      b.   bicuspid valve (mitral valve).
9.   When listening to the heart sounds with a stethoscope, prolapse of the mitral valve sounds like a click at the end of ventricular contraction.
      a.   true   b.   false
10.   Blood is supplied to the heart by the right and left_____ _____.
11.   Cardiac pain is due to
      a.   prolonged contraction of cardiac muscle.   c.   damaged heart valves.
      b.   interruption of blood supply to cardiac muscle. d.   inflammation of heart muscle and valves.
12.   Atrial contraction, while the ventricles relax, followed by ventricular contraction, while the atria relax, is known as the _____ _____.
13.   Heart sounds are a result of
      a.   blood entering the atria in large volumes.   c.   contraction of the myocardium.
      b.   opening and closing of heart valves.   d.   changes in the blood flow rate through the chambers of the heart.
14.   A mass of merging cells that function as a unit is called
      a.   smooth muscle.   c.   the sinoatrial node.
      b.   functional syncytium.   d.   the cardiac conduction system.
15.   The cells that initiate the stimulus for contraction of the heart muscle are located in the
      a.   sinoatrial node.   c.   Purkinje fibers.
      b.   atrioventricular node.   d.   bundle of His.
16.   A recording of the electrical changes that occur in the myocardium during the cardiac cycle is a(n) _____.
17.   In the recording described in question 16, atrial contraction is represented by the
      a.   P wave.   c.   T wave.
      b.   QRS complex.   d.   U wave.
18.   The effect of an increase of parasympathetic nerve impulses on the heart is to (decrease, increase) the heart rate.
19.   Abnormalities in the concentration of which of the following ions is likely to interfere with contraction of the heart?
      a.   chloride   c.   calcium
      b.   potassium   d.   sodium

20. When the smooth muscle of the artery contracts, the action is called _____.

21. Fatty materials, particularly cholesterol, form deposits called _____ on the inner walls of arteries when the condition _____ occurs.

22. The vessel that participates directly in the exchange of substances between the cell and the blood is the

   a. arteriole.   c. capillary.

   b. artery.   d. venule.

23. The amount of blood that flows into capillaries is regulated by

   a. constriction and dilation of capillaries.   c. the amount of intercellular tissue.

   b. arterioles.   d. precapillary sphincters.

24. The transport mechanisms used by the capillaries are _____, _____, and _____.

25. Blood pressure is highest in

   a. an artery.   c. a capillary.

   b. an arteriole.   d. a vein.

26. Plasma proteins help retain water in the blood by maintaining

   a. osmotic pressure.   c. a vacuum.

   b. hydrostatic pressure.

27. The middle layer of the walls of veins differs from that of the arteries in that

   a. it contains more connective tissue.   c. this layer is thicker in the vein.

   b. it contains less smooth muscle.   d. it contains some striated muscle.

28. Blood in veins is kept flowing in one direction by the presence of _____.

29. The maximum pressure in the artery, occurring during ventricular contraction, is

   a. diastolic pressure.   c. mean arterial pressure.

   b. systolic pressure.   d. pulse pressure.

30. The amount of blood pushed out of the ventricle with each contraction is called _____ _____.

31. List the four factors that influence blood pressure.

32. Starling's law is related to which of the following cardiac structures?

   a. interventricular septum   c. muscle fibers

   b. conduction system   d. heart valves

33. When the pressoreceptors in the aorta and carotid artery sense an increase in blood pressure, the medulla relays (sympathetic, parasympathetic) impulses.

34. Peripheral resistance is maintained by increasing or decreasing the size of

   a. capillaries.   c. venules.

   b. arterioles.

35. Venous blood flow is maintained by all but which of the following factors?

   a. blood pressure   c. vasoconstriction of veins

   b. skeletal muscle contraction   d. respiratory movements

36. Which of the following vessels carries deoxygenated blood?

   a. aorta   c. basilar artery

   b. innominate artery   d. pulmonary artery

37. The pulmonary veins enter the _____ _____.

38. List the arteries which originate from the arch of the aorta.

39. The abdominal aorta ends with the right and left _____ _____ arteries.

STUDY ACTIVITIES

I. Aids to Understanding Words

Define the following word parts. (p. 324)

brady-

diastol-

-gram

papill-

syn-

systol-

tachy-

II. 13.1 Introduction (p. 324)

A.   What is the function of the cardiovascular system?

III. 13.2 Structure of the Heart (pp. 325–330)

A.   Describe the precise location of the heart. (p. 325)

B.   Answer these questions concerning the coverings of the heart. (pp. 325–326)

1.   The heart is enclosed by a double-layered _____.

2.   What is the function of the fluid in the pericardial space?

3.   Describe the pathological events of pericarditis.

C.   Answer these questions concerning the wall of the heart. (p. 326)

1.   Label these structures in the accompanying illustration: epicardium, myocardium, endocardium, fibrous pericardium, parietal pericardium, pericardial cavity, coronary blood vessel.

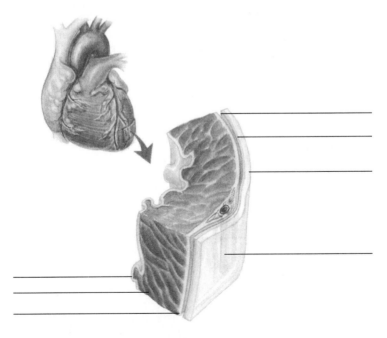

2. Describe the function of each labeled portion of the wall of the heart.

D. Answer these questions concerning heart chambers and valves. (pp. 326–327)
   1. List the chambers of the heart.

   2. Label these structures in the accompanying illustration: right and left ventricles, right and left atria, superior and inferior venae cavae, aorta, tricuspid valve, pulmonary valve, aortic valve, bicuspid valve, right and left pulmonary veins, right and left pulmonary arteries, chordae tendineae, papillary muscles, interventricular septum, pulmonary trunk, opening of coronary sinus.

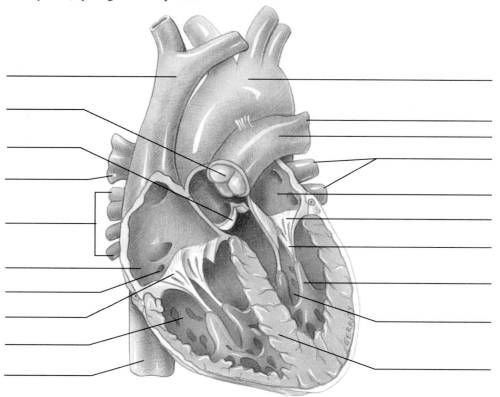

   3. What vessels bring blood to the right atrium?

   4. What vessels bring blood to the left atrium?

E. Trace the path of the blood through the heart. Include all valves. (pp. 328–329)

F. What is mitral valve prolapse? (p. 327)

g.   The cells of the heart are supplied with blood via the _____ _____. (p. 329)

h.   What happens when the heart muscle is deprived of oxygen? (p. 329)

i.   Compare myocardial infarction and angina pectoris. (p. 329)

IV.   **13.3 Heart Actions (pp. 330–337)**

A.   Answer these questions concerning the cardiac cycle. (pp. 330–332)

    1.   What events make up a cardiac cycle?

    2.   What produces the heart sounds heard with a stethoscope?

B.   Describe the characteristics of cardiac muscle fibers. (p. 332)

C.   Answer these questions concerning the cardiac conduction system. (pp. 332–334)

    1.   Label the parts of the cardiac conduction system in the accompanying illustration: interatrial septum, S-A node, A-V node, A-V bundle, Purkinje fibers, interventricular septum, left bundle branch.

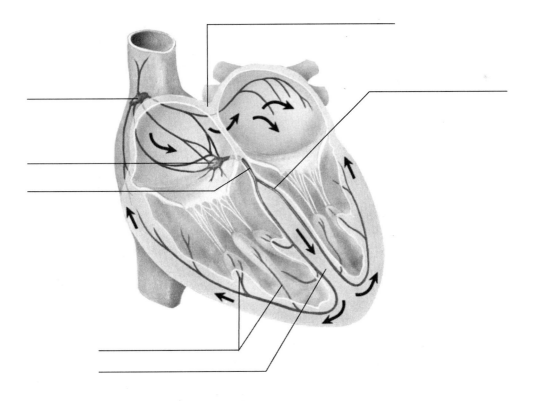

2. Trace an impulse through the cardiac conduction system.

D. Answer these questions concerning the electrocardiogram. (pp. 335–336)
1. A recording of electrical changes in the myocardium is a(n) _____.
2. What events in the cardiac cycle are represented by each of the following: P wave, QRS complex, T wave?

E. Answer these questions concerning regulation of the cardiac cycle. (pp. 336–337)
1. How is the heart regulated by autonomic reflexes?

2. How is the heart affected by potassium and calcium?

V. 13.4 Blood Vessels (pp. 337–342)

A. Answer these questions concerning the cardiovascular system and arteries. (p. 337)
1. Describe the closed circuit formed by blood vessels.

2. What is the structure of the wall of arteries?

3. How is the structure of arterioles different from that of arteries?

4. Describe the changes in arteries that occur with atherosclerosis. (p. 340)

B. Answer these questions concerning capillaries. (pp. 338–341)
1. What is the structure of capillaries?

2. What determines the density of capillaries within tissue?

3. How is the distribution of blood in the various capillary pathways regulated?

4.   What is the blood-brain barrier?

5.   Describe the following transport mechanisms in the capillary.
      filtration

      osmosis

      diffusion

C.   Answer these questions concerning veins. (p. 341)
      1.   What is the structure of a vein?

      2.   In what ways is this different from the structure of an artery?

      3.   How do veins function as a blood reservoir?

VI.   13.5 Blood Pressure (pp. 342–346)

A.   Answer these questions concerning arterial blood pressure. (p. 342)
      1.   What is blood pressure?

      2.   What cardiac events are related to systolic and diastolic arterial pressure?

      3.   What is the pulse?

B.   How do each of the following factors influence arterial blood pressure? (pp. 343–344)
      heart action

      blood volume

      peripheral resistance

      viscosity

C.	Answer these questions concerning control of blood pressure. (pp. 344–346)

    1.	How is cardiac output calculated?

    2.	Discuss the mechanical, neural, and chemical factors that affect cardiac output.

    3.	How is peripheral resistance regulated?

D.	How do factors such as skeletal muscle contraction, breathing, movements, and vasoconstriction of veins influence venous blood flow? (p. 346)

## VII.	13.6 Paths of Circulation (p. 346)

A.	Trace a drop of blood through the pulmonary circuit.

B.	Trace a drop of blood through the systemic circuit.

## VIII.	Clinical Focus Question

Your father has just returned from his annual physical and says, "I have nothing to worry about. My heart is fine. I'm just a little overweight, and my blood pressure is a little high." How would you respond to his comments?

1.	What information about high blood pressure is important for your father to understand?

2.	What lifestyle changes may be helpful for your father to control his blood pressure?

When you have finished the study activities to your satisfaction, retake the mastery test and compare your results with your initial attempt. If you are not satisfied with your performance, repeat the appropriate study activities.

## CHAPTER 14

LYMPHATIC SYSTEM AND IMMUNITY

OVERVIEW

The lymphatic system has two major functions: it helps maintain fluid balance in the tissues of the body, and it has a major role in the defense against infection. This chapter describes the general functions of the lymphatic system (objective 1). In the discussion of fluid balance, it describes the major lymphatic pathways, and lymph formation and circulation (objectives 2–4). In describing the defense function, it explains lymph nodes and their functions (objective 5). Innate and adaptive immunity and the functions of the thymus, spleen, lymphocytes, and immunoglobulins (objectives 6–10) are discussed. Various types of immune responses—primary and secondary responses, active and passive responses, allergic reactions, tissue rejection reactions and formation, activation and immune function of lymphocytes (objectives 9–13)—are also explained.

Study of the lymphatic system completes the knowledge of how fluid is transported to and away from tissues. Knowledge of the immune mechanisms of the lymphatic system is the basis for understanding how the body defends itself against specific kinds of threats.

CHAPTER OBJECTIVES

After you have studied this chapter, you should be able to:

14.1   Introduction

      1. Describe the general functions of the lymphatic system.

14.2   Lymphatic Pathways

      2. Identify the locations of the major lymphatic pathways.

14.3   Tissue Fluid and Lymph

      3. Describe how tissue fluid and lymph form, and explain the function of lymph.

14.4   Lymph Movement

      4. Explain how lymphatic circulation is maintained.

14.5   Lymph Nodes

      5. Describe a lymph node and its major functions.

14.6   Thymus and Spleen

      6. Discuss the functions of the thymus and spleen.

14.7   Body Defenses against Infection

      7. Distinguish between innate (nonspecific) and adaptive (specific) defenses and provide examples of each.

14.8   Nonspecific Defenses

      8. List six innate body defense mechanisms, and describe the action of each mechanism.

14.9   Adaptive Defenses (Specific) or Immunity

      9. Explain how two major types of lymphocytes are formed and activated, and how they function in immune mechanisms.

    10. Name the major types of immunoglobulins and discuss their origins and actions.

    11. Distinguish between primary and secondary immune responses.

    12. Distinguish between active and passive immunity.

    13. Explain how allergic reactions, tissue rejection reactions, and autoimmunity arise from immune mechanisms.

FOCUS QUESTION

Your entire family has had bronchitis for the past week, but despite close contact with them you have not become ill. How has your lymphatic system helped you to avoid contracting this infection?

MASTERY TEST

Now take the mastery test. Do not guess. As soon as you complete the test, correct it. Note your successes and failures so that you can read the chapter to meet your learning needs.

1. Excess fluid in interstitial spaces is carried away by _____ vessels.

2. The smallest vessels in the lymphatic system are called _____ _____. The largest vessels are called _____ _____.

3. The largest lymph vessel is the
   a. lumbar trunk.
   b. thoracic duct.
   c. lymphatic duct.
   d. intestinal trunk.

4. Lymph rejoins the blood and becomes part of the plasma in the
   a. lymph nodes.
   b. right and left subclavian veins.
   c. inferior and superior venae cavae.
   d. right atrium.

5. Tissue fluid originates from
   a. the cytoplasm of cells.
   b. lymph fluid.
   c. blood plasma.

6. The function(s) of lymph is(are) to
   a. recapture small protein molecules lost in the capillary bed.
   b. form tissue fluid.
   c. transport foreign particles to lymph nodes.
   d. recapture electrolytes.

7. The mechanisms that move lymph through lymph vessels are similar to those that move blood through (arteries, veins).

8. Obstruction of the flow of lymph leads to _____.

9. Lymph nodes are shaped like
   a. almonds.
   b. peas.
   c. beans.
   d. convex disks.

10. Lymph nodes contain dense masses of
    a. epithelial tissue.
    b. cilia.
    c. oocytes.
    d. lymphocytes.

11. The thymus is located in the
    a. posterior neck.
    b. thorax.
    c. upper abdomen.
    d. left pelvis.

12. The thymus produces a substance called _____, which seems to stimulate the maturation of _____ cells.

13. The largest of the lymphatic organs is the _____.

14. Which of the following statements about the spleen is(are) true?
    a. The spleen is located in the lower left quadrant of the abdomen.
    b. The spleen functions in the body's defense against infection and as a reservoir for blood.
    c. The structure of the spleen is exactly like that of a lymph node.
    d. Splenic pulp contains large phagocytes on the lining of its venous sinuses.

15. Agents that enter the body and cause disease are called _____.

16. The skin is an example of which of the following body defenses against infection?
    a. immunity
    b. inflammation
    c. mechanical barrier
    d. phagocytosis

17. Which of the following characteristics of the stomach enable it to act as a chemical barrier?
    a. low pH
    b. presence of lysozyme
    c. presence of amylase
    d. presence of pepsin

18. List the four major symptoms of inflammation. _____

9.   Phagocytes that remain fixed in position within various organs are called

a.   neutrophils.   c.   macrophages.

b.   monocytes.

20.   The resistance to specific foreign agents in which certain cells recognize the foreign substances and act to destroy them is

_____   _____.

21.   Some undifferentiated lymphocytes migrate to the _____   _____
where they undergo changes and are then called T lymphocytes.

22.   Foreign substances to which lymphocytes respond are called _____ _____.

23.   T cells and B cells seem to be able to recognize specific foreign proteins because

a.   of changes in the nucleus of these lymphocytes.   c.   there are changes in the permeability of the
cell membrane of these lymphocytes.

b.   the cytoplasm of the T cell and B cell is altered.

d.   of the presence of receptor molecules on T cells
and B cells that fit the molecules of antigens.

24.   T cells attach themselves to antigen-bearing cells and interact directly in a response called_____

_____.

25.   B lymphocytes respond to foreign protein by

a.   phagocytosis.   c.   producing antigens.

b.   interacting directly with pathogens.   d.   producing antibodies.

26.   The three most abundant types of immunoglobulins are _____, _____,

_____.

27.   Antibodies can react to antigens by activating a set of enzymes called _____ to attack the antigens.

28.   T cells require the presence of a(n) _____   _____ before they can

become activated.

29.   In which of the following ways are primary and secondary immune responses different?

a.   Primary responses are more important than   c.   A primary response is a direct response to
secondary responses.   an antigen; a secondary response is indirect.

b.   Primary responses produce more antibodies than   d.   A primary response is the initial response to
secondary responses.   an antigen; a secondary response is all
subsequent responses to that antigen.

30.   A person who receives ready-made antibodies develops artificially acquired _____ immunity.

31.   An individual with special abilities to carry on abnormal immune reactions against usually harmless substances is said
to have

a.   an increased potential for cancer.   c.   a collagen disease.

b.   an allergic reaction.

32.   The immune cells targeted by the human immunodeficiency virus are _____ and

_____   _____   _____.

33.   A common problem following organ transplant is _____   _____

_____.

STUDY ACTIVITIES

I.   Aids to Understanding Words

Define the following word parts. (p. 361)

gen-   inflamm-

humor-   nod-

immun-   patho-

II. 14.1 Introduction (p. 361)

A.   Describe the similarities between the lymphatic system and the cardiovascular system. (p. 361)

B.   What are the functions of the lymphatic system? (p. 361)

III. 14.2 Lymphatic Pathways (pp. 361–362)

A.   What are the components of a lymphatic pathway? (pp. 361–362)

B.   Lymph enters the venous system and becomes part of plasma just before the _____

   _____.

IV. 14.3 Tissue Fluid and Lymph (pp. 362–363)

A.   How is tissue fluid formed? Include the composition of tissue fluid and transport mechanisms used. (p. 363)

B.   How is lymph formed, and how is lymph formation related to tissue fluid formation? (p. 363)

C.   What is the function of lymph? (p. 363)

V. 14.4 Lymph Movement (p. 364)

A.   Describe the forces responsible for the circulation of lymph.

B.   Trace the flow of lymph from the lymph capillaries to the sub clavian veins.

C.   What causes edema?

VI.   14.5 Lymph Nodes (pp. 364–365)

A.   Label these structures in the accompanying illustration: afferent vessel, sinus, nodule, efferent vessel, hilum, capsule, artery, and vein. In addition, indicate the direction of lymph flow through the lymph node. (p. 364)

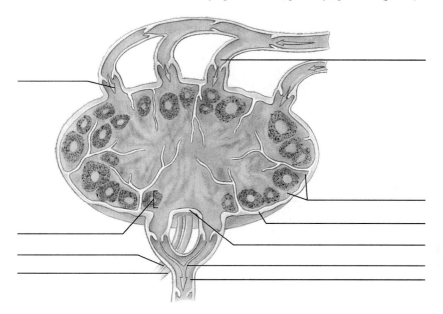

B.   Trace the flow of lymph from the lymph capillaries to the sub clavian veins.

C.   What is the function of lymph nodes? (p. 365)

D.   What is the function of macrophages? (p. 365)

E.   Inflammation of the lymph nodes is called _____. (p. 365)

VII.   14.6 Thymus and Spleen (pp. 365–367)

A.   Describe the location and function of the thymus gland. (p. 365)

B.   Answer these questions concerning the spleen. (p. 367)
    1.   Where is the spleen located?

Label these structures in the accompanying illustration: spleen, capsule, capillary, connective tissue, venous sinus, artery of pulp, red pulp, white pulp, splenic artery, splenic vein.

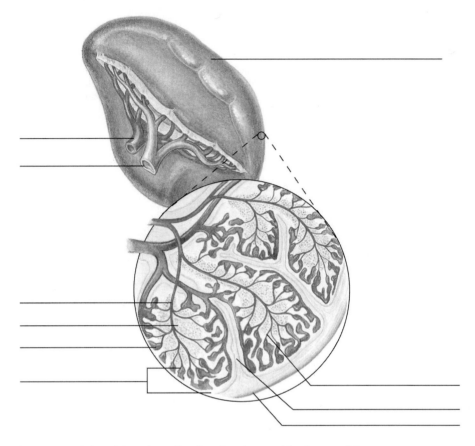

3. What characteristics of the spleen allow it to function as a blood reservoir?

4. What characteristics of the spleen allow it to function in the defense against foreign particles?

VIII. 14.7 Body Defenses against Infection (pp. 367–368)

A. What kinds of agents cause disease?

B. What two major types of defenses prevent disease?

X. 14.8 Innate (Nonspecific) Defenses (pp. 368–369)

A. What is species resistance?

B. What structures function as mechanical barriers?

C. What enzymes help us resist infection?

D. What is interferon, and how does it work?

E. Answer these questions concerning inflammation.
   1. What is inflammation?

   2. Explain the reason for the major symptoms of inflammation.
      redness

      swelling

      heat

      pain

   3. How does fever help protect the body from pathogens?

   4. Describe how inflammation is a defense against infection.

   5. How does the function of reticuloendothelial tissue contribute to the body's defense?

X. 14.9 Adaptive (Specific) Defenses or Immunity (pp. 369–380)

A. Answer these questions concerning specific immunity and the origin of lymphocytes. (p. 369)

1. What is specific immunity?

2. What are antigens?

3. What is a hapten?

4. Where do lymphocytes originate?

5. Why are some lymphocytes called T lymphocytes, while others are called B lymphocytes?

B. Answer these questions concerning the functions of lymphocytes. (p. 369)

1. What are the functions of lymphocytes?

2. How do lymphocytes carry out these functions?

3. Define *cell-mediated immunity* and *antibody-mediated immunity*. Include these mechanisms of action. (pp. 370–373).

4. What are memory cells, and what is their function?

C. Answer these questions concerning types of antibodies. (p. 373)

1. What are antibodies?

2. Fill in the following chart.

Immunoglobulins

Immunoglobulin	Location	Function
Immunoglobulin G		
Immunoglobulin A		
Immunoglobulin M		
Immunoglobulin D		
Immunoglobulin E		

D. Answer these questions concerning primary and secondary specific immune responses. (p. 374)

    1. Define *primary immune response.*

    2. Define *secondary immune response.*

E. Define these terms concerning types of immunity. (pp. 375–376)
naturally acquired active immunity

    artificially acquired active immunity

    artificially acquired passive immunity

    naturally acquired passive immunity

F. Describe the events of an allergic reaction. (pp. 375–377)

G. How is a tissue rejection reaction an immune response? (pp. 377–379)

XI. Clinical Focus Question

AIDS is a communicable disease that has serious economic, moral, and ethical implications. Discuss how this disease attacks the immune system. Identify your personal perspectives on the economic, moral, and ethical issues related to AIDS.

When you have finished the study activities to your satisfaction, retake the mastery test and compare your results with your initial attempt. If you are not satisfied with your performance, repeat the appropriate study activities.

UNIT 5
ABSORPTION AND EXCRETION
CHAPTER 15
DIGESTION AND NUTRITION

OVERVIEW

This chapter is about the digestive system, which processes food so that nutrients can be absorbed and used by cells. It names the organs of the digestive system and describes their locations and functions (objectives 1 and 2). The structure, movement, and digestive mechanisms of the alimentary canal are explained (objectives 3–10). The function and regulation of the secretions of the digestive organs are introduced (objectives 8 and 9). This chapter tells how nutrients are absorbed (objective 11), and explains the defecation reflex (objective 12). This chapter also identifies the major food sources of carbohydrates, lipids, proteins, vitamins, and minerals (objectives 13–16). In addition, it explains the components of an adequate diet (objective 17).

Study of the digestive system helps in understanding how fuel is made available for metabolism, thus enabling cells to function, grow, and reproduce.

CHAPTER OBJECTIVES

After you have studied this chapter, you should be able to:

15.1   Introduction

    1. Describe the general functions of the digestive system.

    2. Name and describe the locations and major parts of the organs of the digestive system.

15.2   General Characteristics of the Alimentary Canal

    3. Describe the structure of the wall of the alimentary canal.

    4. Explain how the contents of the alimentary canal are mixed and moved.

15.3   Mouth

    5. Name the structures of the mouth and describe their functions.

    6. Describe how different types of teeth are adapted for different functions.

    7. List the parts of a tooth.

15.4–15.10   Salivary Glands—Large Intestine

    8. List the enzymes the digestive organs and glands secrete, and describe the function of each.

    9. Describe how digestive secretions are regulated.

    10. Describe the mechanism of swallowing.

    11. Explain how the products of digestion are absorbed.

    12. Describe the defecation reflex.

15.11–15.14   Nutrition and Nutrients

    13. List the major sources of carbohydrates, lipids, and proteins.

    14. Describe how cells use carbohydrates, lipids, and amino acids.

    15. List the fat-soluble and water-soluble vitamins, and summarize the general functions of each vitamin.

    16. List the major minerals and trace elements, and summarize the general functions of each.

    17. Describe an adequate diet.

FOCUS QUESTION

How does the body make the nutrients in a ham sandwich available for absorption by the cells?

MASTERY TEST

Now take the mastery test. Do not guess. As soon as you complete the test, correct it. Note your successes and failures so that you can read the chapter to meet your learning needs.

1. Digestion is the mechanical and chemical breakdown of foods and the absorption of the resulting nutrients by cells

    a. true

    b. false

2. The mouth, pharynx, esophagus, stomach, and large and small intestines make up the _____ _____ of the digestive system.

3. The salivary glands, liver, gallbladder, and pancreas are considered _____ _____.

4. The layer of the wall of the alimentary canal that is formed of surface epithelium and protects underlying tissue while carrying on absorption and secretion is the

    a. mucosa.   c. muscular layer.

    b. submucosa.   d. serosa.

5. The layer of the alimentary tube that keeps the outer surface of the alimentary tube moist and slippery is the

    a. mucosa.   c. muscular layer.

    b. submucosa.   d. serosa.

6. The two basic types of movement of the alimentary canal are_____ movements and _____ movements.

7. Does statement *a* explain statement *b*? _____

    a. Peristalsis is stimulated by stretching the alimentary tube.

    b. Peristalsis acts to move food along the alimentary tube.

8. The tongue is anchored to the floor of the mouth by a fold of membrane called the _____.

9. During swallowing, muscles draw the soft palate and uvula upward to

    a. move food into the esophagus.   c. separate the oral and nasal cavities.

    b. enlarge the area to accommodate a bolus of food.   d. move the uvula from the path of the food bolus.

10. The material that covers the crown of the teeth is

    a. cementum.   c. enamel.

    b. dentin.   d. plaque.

11. Teeth that are chisel shaped and whose function is to bite off pieces of food are

    a. incisors.   c. bicuspids.

    b. cuspids.   d. molars.

12. What parts of a tooth are destroyed by dental caries?

    a. enamel   c. pulp

    b. dentin   d. cementum

13. Which of the following is *not* a function of saliva?

    a. cleanses mouth and teeth   c. helps in formation of food bolus

    b. dissolves chemicals necessary to tasting food   d. begins digestion of protein

14. Stimulation of salivary glands by parasympathetic nerves will (increase, decrease) production of saliva.

5.   The salivary glands that secrete amylase are the
       a.   submaxillary glands.   c.   sublingual glands.
       b.   parotid glands.

6.   When food enters the esophagus, it is transported to the stomach by a movement called _____.

7.   The area of the stomach that acts as a temporary storage area is the
       a.   cardiac region.   c.   body region.
       b.   fundic region.   d.   pyloric region.

8.   The chief cells of the gastric glands secrete
       a.   mucus.   c.   digestive enzymes.
       b.   hydrochloric acid.   d.   potassium chloride.

19.   The digestive enzyme pepsin secreted by gastric glands begins the digestion of
       a.   carbohydrates.   c.   fats.
       b.   protein.

20.   The intrinsic factor secreted by the stomach aids in the absorption of _____
       _____ from the small intestine.

21.   The release of gastrin is stimulated by the
       a.   parasympathetic nervous system.   c.   sight and smell of food.
       b.   presence of alkaline substances.   d.   presence of such substances as protein,
                                                                  caffeine, and alcohol.

22.   Gastric ulcers are considered to be
       a.   a disease of stress.   c.   an endocrine disorder.
       b.   an infectious disease.   d.   a product of overactive parietal cells.

23.   The presence of food in the small intestine (inhibits, increases) gastric secretion.

24.   The semifluid paste formed in the stomach by mixing food and gastric secretions is _____.

25.   The foods that stay in the stomach the longest are high in
       a.   fats.   c.   carbohydrates.
       b.   protein.

26.   Pancreatic enzymes travel along the pancreatic duct and empty into the
       a.   duodenum.   c.   ileum.
       b.   jejunum.

27.   Which of the following enzymes is(are) present in secretions of the mouth, stomach, and pancreas?
       a.   amylase   c.   trypsin
       b.   lipase   d.   lactase

28.   Which of the following is(are) secreted by the pancreas in an inactive form and is(are) activated by a duodenal
       enzyme?
       a.   nuclease   c.   chymotrypsin
       b.   trypsin   d.   carboxypeptidase

29.   The secretions of the pancreas are (acid, alkaline).

30.   The liver is located in the_____ _____ quadrant of the abdomen.

31.   The liver's most vital functions are related to metabolism of
       a.   carbohydrates.   c.   cholesterol.
       b.   fats.   d.   protein.

32.   Type A hepatitis is transmitted by
       a.   ingestion of food contaminated by feces.
       b.   transfusion with blood contaminated by the hepatitis virus.
       c.   use of improperly cleaned needles.
       d.   sexual activity.

33. Which of the following substances are *not* stored in the liver?

    a.   vitamins A and D   c.   iron

    b.   protein   d.   water-soluble vitamins

34. Phagocytic cells found in the inner linings of the sinusoids of the liver are _____ cells.

35. The only substances in bile that have a digestive function are _____

_____.

36. The function(s) of the gallbladder is(are) to

    a.   store bile.   c.   activate bile.

    b.   secrete bile.   d.   concentrate bile.

37. The gallbladder is stimulated to release bile by the hormone _____.

38. Which of the following is(are) the function(s) of bile?

    a.   emulsification of fat globules   c.   increase of solubility of amino acids

    b.   absorption of fats   d.   absorption of fat-soluble vitamins

39. List the portions of the small intestine: _____, _____, and

_____.

40. The velvety appearance of the lining of the small intestine is due to the presence of

    a.   cilia.   c.   mucus secreted by the small intestine.

    b.   villi.   d.   capillaries.

41. The small intestine absorbs (most, few) of the products of digestion.

42. Digestive enzymes and mucus (are, are not) secreted by the small intestine.

43. Peristaltic rush in the small intestine results in _____.

44. The small intestine joins the large intestine at the _____.

45. The only significant secretion of the large intestine is

    a.   potassium.   c.   chyme.

    b.   mucus.   d.   water.

46. The only nutrients normally absorbed in the large intestine are _____ and

_____.

47. The defecation reflex can be initiated by

    a.   holding a deep breath.   c.   contracting the abdominal wall muscles.

    b.   seeing and smelling food.   d.   sensing fullness in the abdomen.

48. The most abundant substance in feces is _____.

49. Nutrients, such as amino acids and fatty acids, that are necessary for health but cannot be synthesized in adequate amounts by the body are called _____ _____.

50. Carbohydrates are ingested in such foods as

    a.   meat and seafood.   c.   butter and margarine.

    b.   bread and pasta.   d.   bacon.

51. A carbohydrate that cannot be broken down by human digestive enzymes and that facilitates muscle activity in the alimentary tube is _____.

52. Glucose can be stored as glycogen in the

    a.   blood plasma.   c.   connective tissue.

    b.   muscles.   d.   liver.

53. The organ most dependent on an uninterrupted supply of glucose is the

    a.   heart muscle.   c.   adrenal gland.

    b.   liver.   d.   brain.

54. An essential fatty acid that cannot be synthesized by the body is _____

_____.

55. A lipid that furnishes molecular components for the synthesis of sex hormones and some adrenal hormones is

_____.

6. Proteins function as

   a. enzymes that regulate metabolic reactions.   c. energy supplies.

   b. promoters of calcium absorption.   d. structural materials in cells.

7. Proteins are absorbed and transported to cells as _____ _____.

8. A protein that contains adequate amounts of the essential amino acids is called a _____ protein.

9. The most abundant minerals in the body are _____ and _____.

10. Iron is associated with the body's ability to transport _____.

STUDY ACTIVITIES

I. Aids to Understanding Words

Define the following word parts. (p. 386)

aliment-

chym-

decidu-

gastr-

hepat-

lingu-

nutri-

peri-

pyl-

vill-

II. 15.1 Introduction (p. 386)

A. Define *digestion.* (p. 386)

B.   Label the illustration of the digestive system. (p. 387)

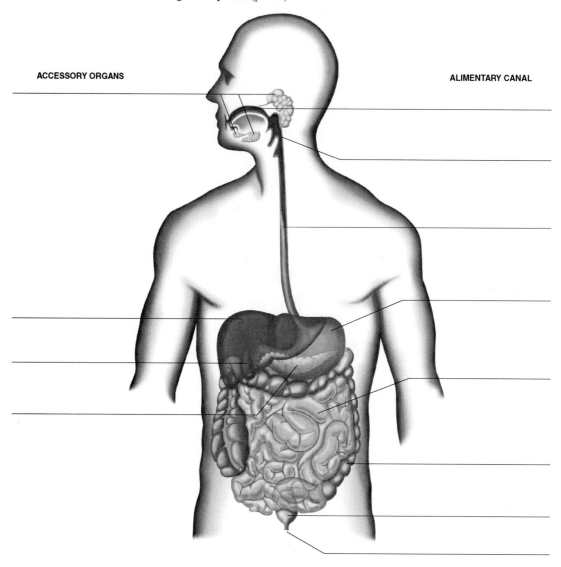

ACCESSORY ORGANS

ALIMENTARY CANAL

III. 15.2 General Characteristics of the Alimentary Canal (pp. 386–387)

A.   Fill in the following table. (p. 386)

Structure and function of the alimentary tube

	Structure	Function
Mucous membrane		
Submucosa		
Muscular layer		
Serous layer		

B.   The two types of movement of the alimentary tube are _____ and

_____. (p. 387) What is peristalsis?

V.   **15.3 Mouth (pp. 388–392)**

A.   What are the functions of the mouth? (p. 388)

B.   What is the function of the tongue? (p. 388)

C.   Answer these questions concerning the palate. (pp. 388–390)

   1.   What are the parts of the palate?

   2.   What is the function of the palate?

   3.   What is the function of the palatene tonsils?

D.   In the accompanying illustration, label the crown, root, enamel, dentin, gingiva, pulp cavity, cementum, alveolar bone, root canal, and periodontal ligament. (p. 392)

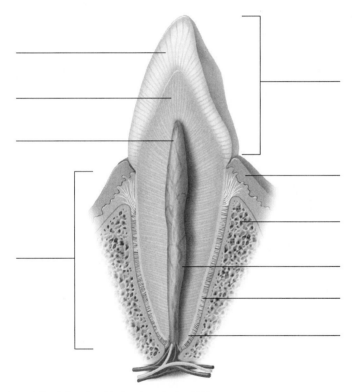

E.   Describe the function of the following kinds of teeth. (p. 391)

   incisors

   cuspids

   bicuspids

   molars

F.   How can individuals best care for their teeth? (p. 392)

G.   The teeth are attached to the jaw by the _____ _____.

V. 15.4 Salivary Glands (pp. 392–393)

A.   Answer these questions concerning salivary glands and their secretions. (p. 392)

   1.   What is the function of salivary glands?

B.   Fill in the following table. (pp. 392–393)

Salivary glands

Glands	Location of the glands	Secretion
Parotid		
Submandibular		
Sublingual		

VI. 15.5 Pharynx and Esophagus (pp. 393–394)

A.   Describe the nasopharynx, oropharynx, and laryngopharynx. (p. 393)

B.   List the events of swallowing. (pp. 393–394)

C.   Describe the structure and functions of the esophagus. (p. 394)

VII. 15.6 Stomach (pp. 395–397)

A.   Answer these questions concerning the stomach and its parts. (p. 395)

   1.   What are the functions of the stomach?

2.   Label the indicated regions of the stomach, and identify the function of each region: fundic region, cardiac region, body, pyloric region, pyloric canal, duodenum, pyloric sphincter, rugae, esophagus, lower esophageal sphincter.

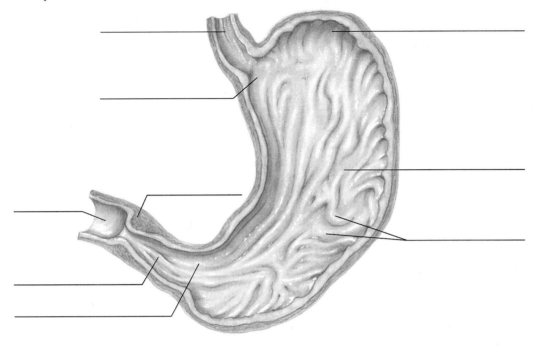

B.   Fill in the following table. (pp. 395–397)

Secretions of gastric gland

Cell type	Secretions	Function and action
Mucous cell		
Chief cell		
Parietal cell		

C.   What substances are absorbed from the stomach? (p. 397)

D.   Answer these questions concerning filling and emptying actions. (p. 397)
    1.   What is chyme, and how is it produced?

    2.   What factors affect the rate at which the stomach empties?

    3.   Describe the vomiting mechanism.

VIII.   15.7 Pancreas (pp. 397–399)

A.   Where is the pancreas located? (p. 397)

B.   Answer these questions concerning pancreatic juice. (pp. 397–399)

1.   Describe the action of the following pancreatic enzymes.

amylase

lipase

trypsin

chymotrypsin

carboxypeptidase

2.   What substance makes the pancreatic juice alkaline?

3.   How does secretin affect pancreatic juice?

4.   What is the function of cholecystokinin?

5.   How is the release of pancreatic enzymes regulated?

IX.   15.8 Liver (pp. 399–404)

A.   1.   Describe the location of the liver. (pp. 399–401)

2.   The liver is divided into _____ lobes.
3.   The functional units of the liver are the _____.
4.   Describe the structure of a hepatic lobule.

5.   The hepatic portal vein brings blood to the liver from the _____ _____.
6.   The large macrophages found in the inner linings of the hepatic sinusoids are _____ _____.
7.   Secretions from the hepatic cells are collected in _____ _____ which converge to form

_____ _____.
8.   Describe the digestive function of the liver.

B.   Fill in the following table regarding hepatitis. (p. 402)

Hepatitis type	Mode of transmission	Patient characteristics
Hepatitis A		
Hepatitis B		
Hepatitis C		
Hepatitis D		
Hepatitis E		
Hepatitis F		
Hepatitis G		

C.   Answer these questions concerning bile. (p. 402)
   1.   Describe the composition of bile.

   2.   Which of the substances in bile is active in the digestive process?

   3.   What is the source of bile pigments?

D.   Answer these questions concerning the gallbladder. (pp. 402–403)
   1.   Where is the gallbladder located?

   2.   How is bile stored?

E.   Describe how bile is released. (p. 403)

F.   Answer these questions concerning the digestive functions of bile salts. (pp. 403–404)
   1.   The digestive function of bile is the _____ of fats.
   2.   Bile salts aid the absorption of _____ _____ and
        _____ .

X.   15.9 Small Intestine (pp. 404–408)

A.   1.   Name and locate the three portions of the small intestine. (p. 404)

2.   The double layer of peritoneal membrane that suspends the jejunum and the ileum from the posterior wall of the abdomen is the _____.

3.   A membrane that can contain and localize infections in the alimentary canal is the _____
_____.

B.   Label these structures in the accompanying illustration, and explain the function of each: lacteal, capillary network, intestinal gland, goblet cells, arteriole, venule, lymph vessel, villus, simple columnar epithelium. (p. 406)

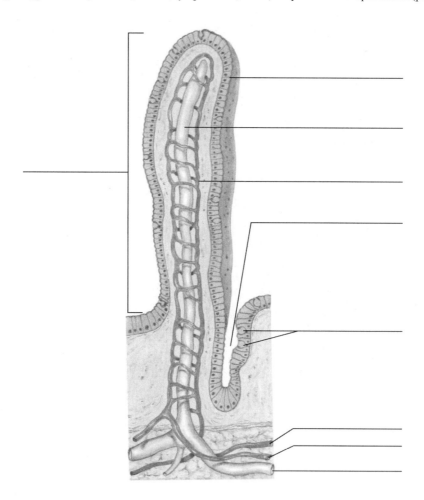

C.   List the secretions of the small intestine, and describe their functions. How are these secretions regulated? (pp. 405–406)

D.   1.   The structures that make absorption in the small intestine so efficient are the _____.
     2.   Carbohydrates are absorbed in the small intestine as _____.
     3.   Protein is absorbed in the small intestine as _____ _____.
     4.   Fat molecules are encased in protein in the small intestine to form _____.
     5.   The transport mechanisms used by the intestinal villi are _____ and _____.

136

XI. 15.10 Large Intestine (pp. 409–412)

A. Answer the questions concerning the large intestine and its parts. (pp. 409–410)

1. Label the parts of the large intestine in the accompanying illustration: vermiform appendix, cecum, ascending colon, transverse colon, descending colon, ileocecal sphincter, serous layer, muscular layer, mucous layer, sigmoid colon, rectum, anal canal, tenia, haustra, oriface of appendix.

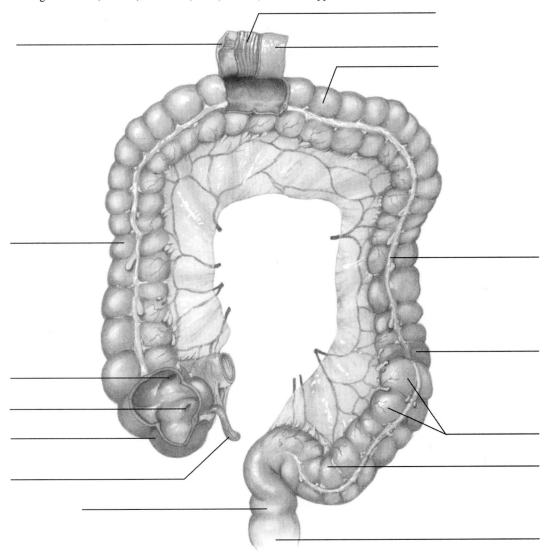

2. How is the structure of the wall of the large intestine different from the structure of the wall of the small intestine?

3. What are hemorrhoids?

B. Answer these questions concerning the functions of the large intestine. (p. 411)

1. What is the function of mucus in the large intestine?

2. What substances are absorbed in the large intestine?

3. What is the role of intestinal bacteria?

C. Answer these questions concerning the movements of the large intestine. (p. 411)
1. Describe the movements of the large intestine.

2. List the events of the defecation reflex.

D. Describe the composition of feces. (pp. 411–412)

XII. 15.11 Nutrition and Nutrients (pp. 412–413)

A. Define nutrition.

B. Nutrients that cannot be synthesized by human cells are called _____ nutrients.

XIII. Carbohydrates (p. 413)

A. Carbohydrates are _____ compounds that are used primarily to supply
_____.

B. In what forms are carbohydrates ingested?

C. In what forms are carbohydrates absorbed?

D. What form of carbohydrate is most commonly used by the cell as fuel?

E. How does cellulose facilitate intestinal function?

F. Identify the areas in which glucose is stored for rapid mobilization.

G. What is the function of carbohydrates?

H. What cells are particularly dependent on a continuous supply of glucose?

What is the estimated daily requirement for carbohydrate?

XIV. **Lipids (pp. 414–415)**

A.   In what forms are lipids usually ingested?

B.   What are the end products of triglyceride digestion?

C.   Describe the role of the liver in the utilization of fats.

D.   An essential fatty acid that cannot be synthesized by the body is _____
_____.

E.   Describe the role of adipose tissue in the utilization of lipids.

F.   What is the function of lipids?

G.   What is the estimated daily requirement for lipids?

XV. **Proteins (pp. 415–416)**

A.   What are the functions of protein?

B.   What is an essential amino acid?

C.   What is the difference between a complete and an incomplete protein?

D.   Why must various sources of vegetable protein be combined in a meal?

E.   What is the estimated daily requirement for protein?

XVI. **Vitamins (pp. 416–418)**

A.   What is a vitamin?

B.   What are the general characteristics of fat-soluble vitamins?

C.   What are the general characteristics of water-soluble vitamins?

D.   Fill in the following table.

Vitamins

Vitamin	Characteristics	Functions	Sources
Vitamin A			
Vitamin D			
Vitamin E			
Vitamin K			
Vitamin B complex *Thiamin (B$_1$)*			
Riboflavin (B$_2$)			
Niacin (nicotinic acid)			
Pyridoxine (B$_6$)			
Pantothenic acid			
Cyanocobalamin (B$_{12}$)			
Folacin (folic acid)			
Biotin			
Ascorbic Acid (vitamin C)			

XVII. Minerals (pp. 418–419)

A.   Describe the general characteristics of minerals.

B.   Fill in the following table.

Major minerals

Mineral	Distribution	Regulatory mechanism	Functions	Sources
Calcium				
Phosphorus				
Potassium				
Sulfur				
Sodium				
Chlorine				
Magnesium				

C.   What is a trace element?

D.   List the nine trace elements, and identify the function of each.

XVIII.   Adequate Diets (p. 418)

A.   1.   What is an adequate diet?

        2.   Define *malnutrition, undernutrition,* and *overnutrition.*

XIX.   Clinical Focus Question

A close friend is planning to be married in three months and tells you she must lose ten pounds before the wedding. She state that she is under a great deal of stress as the wedding approaches. How would you advise her?

Be sure to consider the role of exercise and the effects of stress on nutritional needs.

When you have finished the study activities to your satisfaction, retake the mastery test and compare your results with your initial attempt. If you are not satisfied with your performance, repeat the appropriate study activities.

CHAPTER 16
RESPIRATORY SYSTEM

OVERVIEW

The respiratory system permits the exchange of oxygen, which is needed for cellular metabolism and for carbon dioxide, a by-product of cellular metabolism. This chapter describes the location and function of the organs of the respiratory system and discusses how they contribute to the overall function of the system (objectives 1–3). Respiratory air movements, respiratory volumes and capacities, and how normal breathing is controlled are discussed (objectives 4–7). Gas exchange and transport are explained (objectives 8 and 9).

Air must be taken into the lungs so that oxygen and carbon dioxide can be exchanged. An understanding of these events and how they are controlled is basic to understanding how cells produce energy for life processes.

CHAPTER OBJECTIVES

After you have studied this chapter, you should be able to:

16.1 Introduction
1. List the general functions of the respiratory system.
16.2 Organs of the Respiratory System
2. Name and describe the locations of the organs of the respiratory system.
3. Describe the functions of each organ of the respiratory system.
16.3 Breathing Mechanisms
4. Explain the mechanisms of inspiration and expiration.
5. Name and define each of the lung volumes and respiratory capacities.
16.4 Control of Breathing
6. Locate the respiratory center, and explain how it controls normal breathing.
7. Discuss how various factors affect the respiratory center.
16.5 Alveolar Gas Exchanges
8. Describe the structure and function of the respiratory membrane.
16.6 Gas Transport
9. Explain how air and blood exchange gases and how blood transports these gases.

FOCUS QUESTION

You have climbed three flights of steps to get to your classroom. You then sit quietly in a lecture hall taking notes. How does the respiratory system help maintain your body equilibrium with such different levels of physical activity?

MASTERY TEST

Now take the mastery test. Do not guess. As soon as you complete the test, correct it. Note your successes and failures so that you can read the chapter to meet your learning needs.

1. The process of the atmosphere and body cells exchanging gases is called _____.
2. Match the functions in the first column with the appropriate part of the nose in the second column.

_____ a. warms incoming air   1. mucous membrane
_____ b. traps particulate matter in the air   2. mucus
_____ c. prevents infection   3. cilia
_____ d. moistens air
_____ e. moves nasal secretions to pharynx

3. The pharynx is the cavity behind the mouth, extending from the _____ _____ to the _____.

4. The portions of the larynx that prevent foreign objects from entering the trachea are the
   a. arytenoid cartilages.
   b. glottis.
   c. epiglottis.
   d. hyoid bone.

5. The trachea is maintained in an open position by
   a. cartilaginous rings.
   b. the amount of collagen in the wall.
   c. the tone of smooth muscle in the wall of the trachea.
   d. the continuous flow of air through the trachea.

6. The right and left bronchi arise from the trachea at the
   a. suprasternal notch.
   b. manubrium of the sternum.
   c. fifth thoracic vertebra.
   d. eighth intercostal space.

7. The smallest branches of the bronchial tree are the _____ _____.

8. The serous membrane covering the lungs is the _____ _____.

9. The serous membrane covering the inner wall of the thoracic cavity is the _____ _____.

10. The disease that results in decreased surface area of the respiratory membrane and loss of elasticity in the alveolar walls is _____.

11. The right lung is (larger, smaller) than the left lung.

12. The pressure in the thoracic cavity during inspiration is
    a. greater than atmospheric pressure.
    b. less than atmospheric pressure.
    c. the same as atmospheric pressure.

13. Inspiration occurs after the diaphragm _____, thus (increasing, decreasing) the size of the thorax and (increasing, decreasing) the pressure within the thorax.

14. The other muscles that normally act to change the size of the thorax are the
    a. sternocleidomastoids.
    b. pectorals.
    c. intercostals.
    d. latissimus dorsi.

15. Expansion of the lungs during inspiration is assisted by the surface tension of fluid in the _____ cavity.

16. The surface tension of fluid in the alveoli is decreased by the secretion _____, which prevents collapse of the alveoli.

17. The force responsible for expiration comes mainly from
    a. contraction of intercostal muscles.
    b. change in the surface tension within alveoli.
    c. elastic recoil of tissues in the lung and thoracic wall.
    d. contraction of abdominal muscle to push the diaphragm upward.

18. The amount of air that enters and leaves the lungs during a normal, quiet respiration is the
    a. vital capacity.
    b. inspiratory reserve volume.
    c. total lung capacity.
    d. tidal volume.

19. Normal breathing is controlled by the respiratory center located in the _____.

20. The inflation reflexes are activated by
    a. stretch receptors in the bronchioles and alveoli.
    b. an increase in hydrogen ions.
    c. a decrease in oxygen saturation.
    d. a sudden fall in blood pressure.

21. The strongest stimulus to increase respiratory rate and depth is to increase the blood concentration of _____ _____.

22. The respiratory membrane consists of a single layer of epithelial cells and basement membrane between a(n) _____ and a(n) _____.

23. The rate at which a gas diffuses from one area to another is determined by differences in _____ in the two areas.

24. The pressure of each gas within a mixture is known as its _____

_____.

25. Oxygen is transported to cells by combining with _____.

26. The largest amount of carbon dioxide is transported

    a. dissolved in blood.

    b. combined with hemoglobin.

    c. as bicarbonate.

    d. as carbonic anhydrase.

STUDY ACTIVITIES

I. Aids to Understanding Words

Define the following word parts. (p. 429)

alveol-

bronch-

cric-

epi-

hemo-

II. 16.1 Introduction (p. 429)

Define the following terms related to respiration.

1. Ventilation

2. gas exchange

3. gas transport

4. cellular respiration

III. 16.2 Organs of the Respiratory System (pp. 429–436)

A.   In the accompanying illustration, label these structures: nasal cavity, nostril, pharynx, larynx, trachea, bronchus, right lung, left lung, epiglottis, hard palate, soft palate, oral cavity, esophagus, frontal sinus. (p. 429)

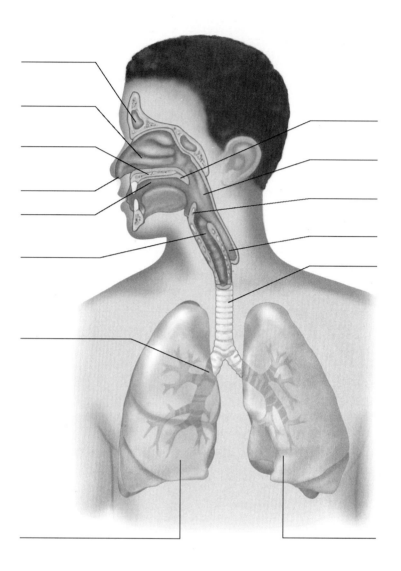

B.   Match the functions in the first column with the appropriate terms in the second column. (pp. 429–430)

_____ 1.   entrap(s) dust   a.   mucous membrane

_____ 2.   lighten(s) skull and provide vocal resonance   b.   mucus

_____ 3.   warms and humidif(y)ies air entering the nose   c.   sinuses

_____ 4.   provide(s) movement to mucus layer   d.   cilia

C.   Describe the location and functions of the paranasal sinuses. (p. 430)

D.   What is the location and function of the pharynx? (p. 431)

E. Answer these questions concerning the larynx. (pp. 431–432)

  1. Identify these structures in the accompanying illustration: hyoid bone, epiglottic cartilage, trachea, thyroid cartilage, cricoid cartilage.

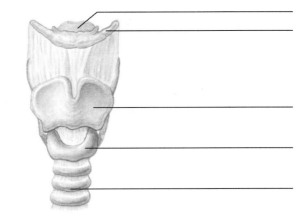

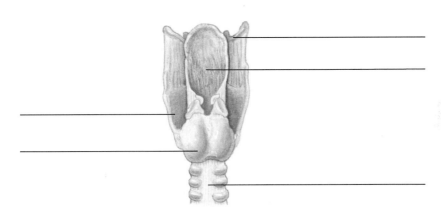

  2. The structure of the larynx that helps close the glottis during swallowing is the _____.

  3. The structures of the larynx that produce sound are the _____.

F. Describe the structure and function of the inner wall of the trachea. (p. 432)

G. Answer these questions concerning the bronchial tree. (pp. 432–434)

1. In the accompanying illustration, label the larynx, trachea, right primary bronchus, secondary bronchus, alveolus, alveolar duct, bronchiole, right superior lobe of lung, right middle lobe of lung, right inferior lobe of lung, left superior lobe of lung, left inferior lobe of lung, terminal bronchiole, tertiary branches.

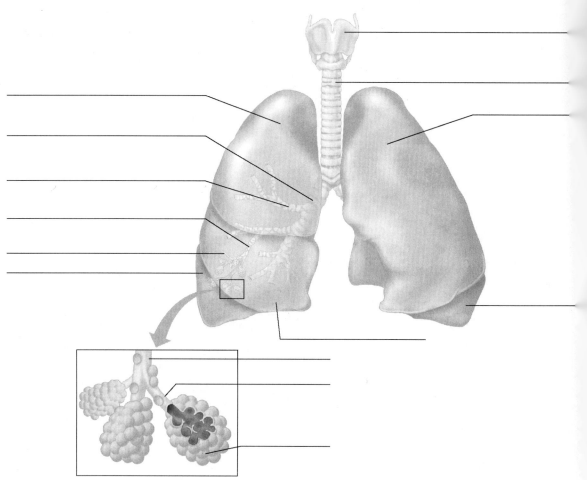

2. What is the function of the alveoli?

H. Answer these questions concerning the lungs. (p. 435)

1. The right lung has _____ lobes, and the left lung has _____ lobes.

2. How is the pleural cavity formed?

IV.   16.3 Breathing Mechanism (pp. 436–441)

A.   Answer these questions concerning inspiration. (pp. 436–437)

    1.   List the events of inspiration.

    2.   Describe the role of surface tension in the pleural cavity and in the alveoli.

    3.   How does surfactant support the function of the alveoli?

B.   List the events of expiration. (pp. 437–438)

C.   Match the terms in the first column with their correct definition in the second column. (pp. 438–439)

    _____ 1.   inspiratory reserve volume

    _____ 2.   expiratory reserve volume

    _____ 3.   residual volume

    _____ 4.   vital capacity

    _____ 5.   total lung capacity

    _____ 6.   tidal volume

    _____ 7.   inspiratory capacity

    _____ 8.   functional residual capacity

    a.   volume of air that remains in the lungs following exhalation of tidal volume

    b.   volume moved in or out of the lungs during quiet respiration

    c.   volume that can be inhaled during forced breathing in addition to tidal volume

    d.   volume that can be exhaled in addition to tidal volume

    e.   volume that remains in the lungs at all times

    f.   maximum air that can be exhaled after taking the deepest possible breath

    g.   total volume of air the lungs can hold

    h.   maximum volume of air that can be inhaled following exhalation of tidal volume

D.   Describe the role of surfactant in neonatal respiration. (p. 437)

V.   16.4 Control of Breathing (pp. 441–443)

A.   List the neural, muscular, skeletal, and pulmonary structures involved in the control of breathing. (pp. 441–442)

B.   Describe the function of the respiratory center in maintaining normal breathing. Include the medullary rhythmicity area, dorsal respiratory group, ventral respiratory group, and pneumotaxic area. (p. 443)

C.   How do chemical factors affect breathing? (p. 443)

VI.   16.5 Alveolar Gas Exchanges (pp. 443–445)

A.   Identify the layers of cells that comprise the respiratory membrane. (p. 443)

B.   Answer these questions concerning diffusion through the respiratory membrane. (pp. 444–445)
        1.   What determines the direction and rate at which gases diffuse from one area to another?

        2.   Define *partial pressure of gas.*

        3.   Use partial pressure of gas to explain the exchange of oxygen and carbon dioxide in the alveoli.

VII.   16.6 Gas Transport (pp. 445–448)

A.   Answer these questions concerning oxygen transport. (p. 445)
        1.   Describe how oxygen is transported to cells.

        2.   Why is oxygen released at the cell?

B.   A gas that interferes with oxygen transport by forming a stable bond with hemoglobin is _____
        _____. (p. 447)

C.   Answer these questions concerning carbon dioxide transport. (pp. 446–448)
        1.   How is carbon dioxide transported away from the cell?

        2.   Why is CO_2 lost in the lung?

III. Clinical Focus Question

. How do the anatomic changes of emphysema affect the physiology of the respiratory system? Be sure to consider changes in the mechanism of breathing, gas exchange, and the control of breathing.

3. What differences would you expect when auscultating a normal lung and an emphysemic lung?

When you have finished the study activities to your satisfaction, retake the mastery test and compare your results with your initial attempt. If you are not satisfied with your performance, repeat the appropriate study activities.

OVERVIEW

The urinary system plays a vital role in maintenance of the internal environment by excreting nitrogenous waste products and by selectively excreting or retaining water and electrolytes. This chapter identifies, locates, and describes the functions of the organs of the urinary system (objectives 1–3). It explains the structure and function of the nephron—the basic unit of function of the kidney (objective 5), traces the pathway of blood through the blood vessels of the kidney, explains how glomerular filtrate is produced, and discusses the role of tubular reabsorption in urine production (objectives 4, 6–8). It also describes the role of tubular secretion in urine formation (objective 9) and discusses the structure of the ureters, urinary bladder, and urethra, and how they function in micturition (objectives 10 and 11).

A study of the urinary system is basic to understanding how the body maintains its chemistry within very narrow limits.

CHAPTER OBJECTIVES

After you have studied this chapter, you should be able to:

17.1   Introduction
    1. Name and list the general functions of the organs of the urinary system.

17.2   Kidneys
    2. Describe the locations and structure of the kidneys.
    3. List the functions of the kidneys.
    4. Trace the pathway of blood through the major vessels within a kidney.
    5. Describe a nephron, and explain the functions of its major parts.

17.3   Urine Formation
    6. Explain how glomerular filtrate is produced, and describe its composition.
    7. Explain the factors that affect the rate of glomerular filtration and how this rate is regulated.
    8. Discuss the role of tubular reabsorption in urine formation.
    9. Define *tubular secretion,* and explain its role in urine formation.

17.4   Urine Elimination
    10. Describe the structure of the ureters, urinary bladder, and urethra.
    11. Explain the process and control of micturition.

FOCUS QUESTION

This afternoon you attended a reception for the new president of the college. You enjoyed the salted nuts, smoked fish, cream puffs, petit fours, and other hors d'oeuvres that were served. How will the urinary system respond to this unusual food intake?

MASTERY TEST

Now take the mastery test. Do not guess. As soon as you complete the test, correct it. Note your successes and failures so that you can read the chapter to meet your learning needs.

1. The functions of the urinary system include:
    a. elimination of nitrogenous wastes and carbon dioxide
    b. control of blood pressure
    c. red blood cell production
    d. regulation of pH.

2. The organ(s) of the urinary system that function primarily to transport urine is(are) the
    a. kidney.
    b. urethra.
    c. ureters.
    d. bladder.

3. The kidneys are located
   a. within the abdominal cavity.
   c. posterior to the parietal peritoneum.
   b. between the twelfth thoracic and third lumbar vertebrae.
   d. just below the diaphragm.

4. The superior end of the ureters is expanded to form the funnel-shaped _____
   _____.

5. A series of small elevations that project into the renal sinus from the substance of the kidney and form the sinus wall are called
   a. renal pyramids.
   c. renal calyces.
   b. the renal medulla.
   d. renal papillae.

6. The blood supply to the nephron is via
   a. the renal artery.
   c. an arciform artery.
   b. an interlobar artery.
   d. afferent arterioles.

7. The structure of the renal corpuscle consists of the
   a. glomerulus.
   c. descending loop of Henle.
   b. glomerular capsule.
   d. proximal convoluted tubule.

8. The transport mechanism used in the glomerulus is
   a. filtration.
   c. active transport.
   b. osmosis.
   d. diffusion.

9. High pressure in the glomerulus is maintained by the diameter of the _____ _____.

10. The control of renin secretion is the function of the _____ apparatus.

11. The end product of kidney function is _____.

12. The fluid formed in the capillary cluster of the nephron is the same as blood plasma except for the absence of
    a. glucose.
    c. bicarbonate ions.
    b. larger molecules of plasma protein.
    d. creatinine.

13. Blood pressure affects urine formation because _____ _____ of the blood is necessary to the transport mechanism used in the glomerulus.

14. How much fluid filters through the glomerulus in a 24-hour period?
    a. 1 ½ quarts
    c. 45 gallons
    b. 2 cups
    d. 5–10 quarts

15. Renin is secreted by the juxtaglomerular cells in response to a fall in
    a. blood pressure.
    c. potassium.
    b. sodium.
    d. all of the above.

16. The kidney enzyme _____ helps regulate _____
    _____.

17. Which of the following substances are present in glomerular filtrate but not in urine?
    a. urea
    c. potassium
    b. sodium
    d. glucose

18. Substances such as sodium ions are reabsorbed in the
    a. proximal convoluted tubule.
    c. descending limb of the loop of Henle.
    b. distal convoluted tubule.
    d ascending limb of the loop of Henle.

19. The permeability of the distal segment of the tubule to water is regulated by
    a. blood pressure.
    c. aldosterone.
    b. ADH.
    d. renin.

20. The mechanism by which greater amounts of a substance may be excreted in urine than were filtered from the plasma in the glomerulus is
   a. tubular absorption.
   b. active transport.
   c. pinocytosis.
   d. tubular secretion.

21. Which of the following substances enter the urine via tubular secretion?
   a. lactic acid
   b. hydrogen ions
   c. amino acids
   d. potassium

22. The normal output of urine for an adult in an hour is
   a. 20–30 cc.
   b. 30–40 cc.
   c. 40–50 cc.
   d. 50–60 cc.

23. Urine is conveyed from the kidney to the bladder via the _____.

24. Urine moves along the ureters via
   a. hydrostatic pressure.
   b. gravity.
   c. peristalsis.

25. Inflammation of the bladder is called _____.

26. The internal floor of the bladder has three openings in a triangular area called the _____.

27. The third layer of the bladder is composed of smooth muscle fibers and is called the
   a. micturition muscle.
   b. detrusor muscle.
   c. urinary muscle.
   d. sympathetic muscle.

28. When stretch receptors in the bladder send impulses along parasympathetic paths, the individual experiences a sensation known as _____.

29. The usual amount of urine voided at one time is about
   a. 50 ml.
   b. 150 ml.
   c. 500 ml.
   d. 1,000 ml.

30. Which of the following structures is under conscious control?
   a. external urethral sphincter
   b. internal urethral sphincter
   c. bladder wall

STUDY ACTIVITIES

I. Aids to Understanding Words

Define the following word parts. (p. 453)

calyc-   mict-
cort-   nephr-
detrus-   papill-
glom-   trigon-

II. 17.1 Introduction (p. 454)

List the functions of the urinary system.

17.2 Kidneys (pp. 454–459)

A.   Identify the parts of the urinary system in the accompanying illustration: kidney, bladder, ureter, aorta, inferior vena cava, hilum, renal artery, renal vein, urethra. (p. 454)

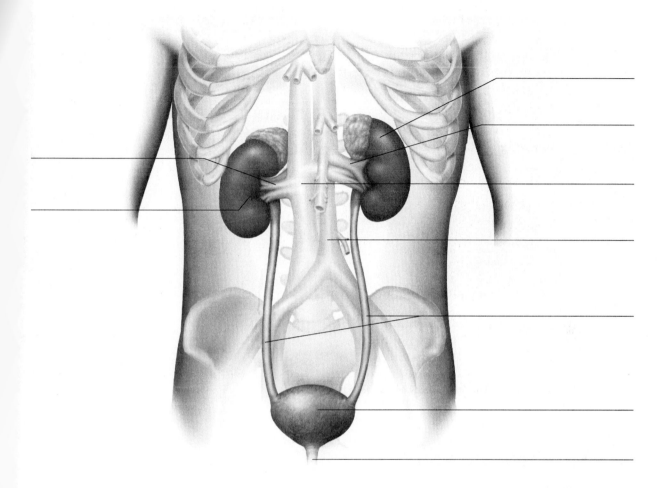

B.   Describe the precise location of the kidneys. (p. 454)

C. Label these structures in the accompanying illustration: renal capsule, renal pelvis, major and minor calyces, renal cortex, renal medulla, renal papilla, renal pyramid, ureter, renal column. (p. 455)

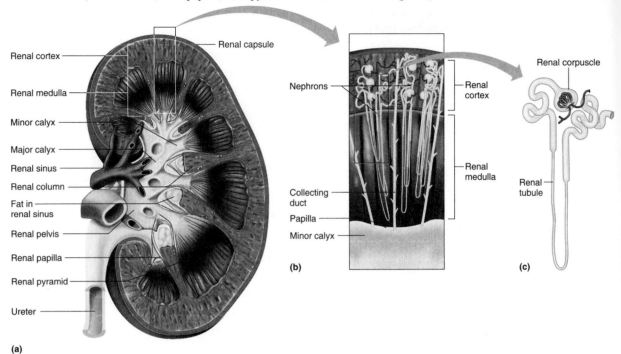

(a)

D. What is the functional unit of the kidney? (p. 454)

E. What are the arterial and venous pathways in the kidney? (p. 455)

F. Describe the structure of a nephron.

G. 1. Blood leaves the glomerulus via the an _____ _____.
    2. Pressure in the glomerulus is maintained partly because the efferent arteriole is (larger, smaller) than the afferent arteriole.
    3. The efferent arterioles branch into a network called the _____ _____ _____.
    4. Blood from the kidney returns to circulation via the _____ _____.

IV. **17.3 Urine Formation (pp. 459–466)**

A. Answer these questions concerning urine formation. (p. 459)
    1. Urine formation begins with _____ _____.
    2. The excess water removed by the first step in urine formation to the venous circulation is returned using _____ _____.
    3. Hydrogen ions are removed from the body using _____ _____.

B. Answer these questions concerning glomerular filtration. (pp. 459–462)
    1. Describe glomerular filtration.

2.   How is glomerular filtration rate affected?

3.   What is the amount and composition of glomerular filtrate?

4.   Why is renin secreted?

5.   Describe the actions of angiotensin I and angiotensin II.

6.   What is the role of atrial natriuretic peptide?

C.   Answer these questions concerning tubular reabsorption. (pp. 462–464)
1.   Explain this statement: Tubular reabsorption is selective. Illustrate it by describing the reabsorption of glucose and amino acids.

2.   Define *renal plasma threshold.*

3.   List the substances reabsorbed by the epithelium of the proximal convoluted tubule.

4.   Describe water and sodium reabsorption in the proximal segment of the renal tubule.

5.   Describe exactly how ADH affects the nephron.

6.   How is urea reabsorbed?

D.   Answer these questions concerning tubular secretion. (p. 464)
1.   What is tubular secretion?

2.   Where are hydrogen ions secreted?

3.   How are potassium ions secreted?

E.   Answer these questions concerning the composition of urine. (p. 466)
        1.   What is the composition of normal urine?

        2.   What is the normal output of urine?

V.   17.4 Urine Elimination (pp. 467–469)

A.   Answer these questions concerning the ureters. (p. 467)
        1.   Describe the location and structure of the ureters.

        2.   How is urine moved through the ureters?

B.   Answer these questions concerning the urinary bladder. (p. 468)
        1.   How does the bladder change as it fills with urine?

        2.   How is urine prevented from spilling back into the ureters?

        3.   Describe the structure of the bladder wall.

C.   Describe the process of micturition. Be sure to include both autonomic and voluntary events. (p. 469)

D.   The tube that conveys urine from the bladder to the outside of the body is the _____.

VI. Clinical Focus Question

A.   Based on renal physiology, what is the electrolyte most important to survival? Explain your answer.

B.   List the possible reasons for finding red blood cells in urine.

C.   What signs and symptoms would you expect to observe in an individual experiencing renal failure?

When you have finished the study activities to your satisfaction, retake the mastery test and compare your results with your initial attempt. If you are not satisfied with your performance, repeat the appropriate study activities.

CHAPTER 18
WATER, ELECTROLYTE, AND ACID-BASE BALANCE

OVERVIEW

This chapter presents the roles of several body systems in maintaining proper concentrations of water and electrolytes. It defines water and electrolyte balance and explains its importance (objective 1). It tells how water enters the body, how water is distributed in various body compartments, and how it leaves the body (objectives 2 and 3). It explains how electrolytes enter and leave the body and how their concentration is regulated (objective 4). Acid-base balance and mechanisms regulating this balance are also described as well as the consequences of imbalance (objectives 5–8).

Water and electrolyte balance affects and is affected by the various chemical interactions of the body. A knowledge of the mechanisms that control fluid and electrolyte concentrations is essential to understanding the nature of the internal environment.

CHAPTER OBJECTIVES

After you have studied this chapter, you should be able to:

18.1   Introduction

1.   Explain water and electrolyte balance, and discuss the importance of this balance.

18.2   Distribution of Body Fluids

2.   Describe how the body fluids are distributed within compartments, how fluid composition differs between compartments, and how fluids move from one compartment to another.

18.3   Water Balance

3.   List the routes by which water enters and leaves the body, and explain the regulation of water intake and output.

18.4   Electrolyte Balance

4.   Explain how electrolytes enter and leave the body and the regulation of electrolyte intake and output.

18.5   Acid-Base Balance

5.   List the major sources of hydrogen ions in the body.

6.   Distinguish between strong and weak acids and bases.

7.   Explain how chemical buffer systems, the respiratory center, and the kidneys minimize changing pH values of the body fluids.

18.6   Acid-Base Imbalances

8.   Describe the causes and consequences of elevation or decrease of body fluid pH.

FOCUS QUESTION

You have eaten a large bowl of salted popcorn while studying and suddenly realize you are very thirsty. Why are you thirsty?

MASTERY TEST

Now take the mastery test. Do not guess. As soon as you complete the test, correct it. Note your successes and failures so that you can read the chapter to meet your learning needs.

1.   *Fluid and electrolyte balance* implies that the quantities of these substances entering the body _____ the quantities leaving the body.

2.   Which of the following statements about fluid and electrolyte balance is(are) true?

a.   Fluid balance is independent of electrolyte balance.

b.   The concentration of an individual electrolyte is the same throughout the body.

c.   Water and electrolytes occur in compartments in which the composition of fluid varies.

d.   Water is evenly distributed throughout the tissues of the body.

3.   More than 60 percent of body fluid occurs within the cells in a compartment called the _____
     fluid compartment.

4.   Blood and cerebrospinal fluid occur in the _____ fluid compartment.

5.   Which of the following electrolytes is(are) most concentrated within the cell?

     a.   sodium   c.   chloride

     b.   bicarbonate   d.   potassium

6.   Plasma leaves the capillary at the arteriole end and enters interstitial spaces because of_____
     pressure.

7.   Fluid returns from the interstitial spaces to the plasma at the venule end of the capillary because of

     _____ pressure.

8.   The most important source of water for the normal adult is

     a.   in the form of beverages.   c.   from oxidative metabolism of nutrients.

     b.   from moist food, such as lettuce and tomatoes.

9.   Thirst is experienced when

     a.   the mucosa of the mouth begins to lose water.   c.   the hypothalamus is stimulated by increasing
                                                                osmotic pressure of extracellular fluid.
     b.   salt concentration in the cell increases.
                                                          d.   the cortex of the brain is stimulated by
                                                               shifts in the concentration of sodium.

10. The primary regulator of water output is

     a.   loss in the feces.   c.   urine production.

     b.   evaporation as sweat.   d.   loss with respiration.

11. The amount of water lost or retained is regulated by

     a.   changes in metabolic rate.   c.   the amount and consistency of feces.

     b.   an increase or decrease in respiratory rate.   d.   an antidiuretic hormone.

12. The primary source of electrolytes is _____ and _____.

13. List three routes by which electrolytes are lost.

14. Sodium and potassium ion concentrations are regulated by the kidneys and the hormone _____.

15. Calcium ion concentration in the plasma is regulated by _____ _____.

16. Acid-base balance is mainly concerned with regulating_____ _____
     concentration.

17. Anaerobic respiration of glucose produces

     a.   carbonic acid.   c.   acetoacetic acid.

     b.   lactic acid.   d.   ketones.

18. The strength of an acid depends on the

     a.   number of hydrogen ions in each molecule.   c.   degree to which molecules ionize in water.

     b.   nature of the inorganic salt.   d.   concentration of acid molecules.

19. A base is a substance that will_____ _____ hydrogen ions.

20. A buffer is a substance that

     a.   returns an acid solution to neutral.   c.   converts strong acids or bases to weak acids
                                                               or bases.
     b.   converts acid solutions to alkaline solutions.
                                                          d.   returns an alkaline solution to neutral.

21. The most important buffer system in plasma and intracellular fluid is the

     a.   bicarbonate buffer.   c.   protein buffer.

     b.   phosphate buffer.

22. The respiratory center controls hydrogen ion concentration by controlling the _____ and
     _____ of respirations.

23.   The slowest acting of the mechanisms that control pH is the
        a.   buffer systems.   c.   kidneys.
        b.   respiratory system.
24.   Factors that increase the concentration of carbonic acid lead to _____acidosis.
25.   Factors that can lead to metabolic acidosis include
        a.   decreased glomerular filtration.   c.   diabetes mellitus.
        b.   pneumonia.   d.   vomiting and diarrhea.

STUDY ACTIVITIES

I.   Aids to Understanding Words

Define the following word parts. (p. 475)

de-   intra-

extra-   neutr-

im-

II.   18.1 Introduction (p. 475)

A.   Define *water* and *electrolyte balance.*

B.   Because electrolytes are dissolved in water, water and electrolyte balance are_____ .

III.   18.2 Distribution of Body Fluids (pp. 475–477)

A.   What is the composition of extracellular fluid? (p. 475)

B.   What is the composition of intracellular fluid? (pp. 475–476)

C.   What mechanisms are responsible for the movement of fluid and electrolytes from one compartment to another? Describe these mechanisms as fully as possible. (pp. 476–477)

IV.   18.3 Water Balance (pp. 477–480)

A.   Answer these questions concerning water intake. (p. 477)
        1.   Water balance exists when gain of water from all sources _____ the total loss of water.
        2.   From what sources is this water derived?

B.   Describe the mechanism that regulates the intake of water. (p. 477)

C.   By what routes is water lost from the body? (p. 480)

D.   The hormone that regulates water balance is _____. How is this accomplished? (p. 480)

E.   Describe the development and symptoms of dehydration. (p. 478)

V.   **18.4 Electrolyte Balance (pp. 480–481)**

A.   Answer these questions concerning electrolyte intake. (p. 480)
         1.   List the electrolytes that are important to cellular function.

         2.   What are the sources of these electrolytes?

B.   List three routes by which electrolytes are lost. (p. 480)

C.   Answer these questions concerning regulation of electrolyte balance. (pp. 480–481)
         1.   What is the role of aldosterone in electrolyte regulation?

         2.   What is the role of parathyroid hormone in electrolyte regulation?

         3.   What is the role of the kidney in electrolyte regulation?

4.   How is the concentration of negatively charged ions regulated?

5.   Describe the causes and symptoms of high and low concentrations of sodium and potassium.

VI.   18.5 Acid-Base Balance (pp. 482–484)

A.   Answer these questions concerning acid-base balance. (p. 482)
   1.   What is an acid?

   2.   What is a base?

   3.   What is acid-base balance?

B.   List and describe the sources of hydrogen ions in the body. (p. 482)

C.   What is the difference between a strong acid or base and a weak acid or base? (p. 482)

D.   Answer these questions concerning regulation of hydrogen ion concentration. (pp. 482–484)
   1.   How is hydrogen ion concentration regulated by acid-base buffer systems?

   2.   Describe how this works with the bicarbonate buffer system, the phosphate buffer system, and the protein buffer system.

   3.   How does the respiratory center regulate hydrogen ion concentration?

4. How do the kidneys help regulate hydrogen ion concentration?

5. How do these mechanisms differ from each other, especially with respect to speed of action?

VII. Acid-Base Imbalances (pp. 484–487)

A.   What is the normal pH value? (p. 484)

B.   Compare metabolic and respiratory acidosis. (pp. 484–486)

C.   Compare metabolic and respiratory alkalosis. (pp. 486–487)

VIII. Clinical Focus Question

A.   How is environmental temperature related to water and electrolyte balance?

B.   How would you maintain water and electrolyte balance in hot weather for
    1.   infants?

    2.   young athletic adults?

    3.   middle-aged sedentary adults?

    4.   elderly adults who live alone?

When you have finished the study activities to your satisfaction, retake the mastery test and compare your results with your initial attempt. If you are not satisfied with your performance, repeat the appropriate study activities.

OVERVIEW

This chapter explains reproductive systems—unique systems because they are essential to the survival of the species rather than to the survival of the individual. The chapter explains the structure and functions of the male and female reproductive systems (objectives 1–4, 6, 7). It also describes the hormonal events that control the male and female reproductive systems, as well as the major events of the menstrual cycle (objectives 5, 8, 9). The structure of the mammary glands is described (objective 10). The relative effectiveness of several methods of birth control is discussed (objective 11). Symptoms of sexually transmitted diseases are listed (objective 12).

Understanding the processes of sexual function contributes to an understanding of humans as sexual beings.

CHAPTER OBJECTIVES

After you have studied this chapter, you should be able to:

19.1   Introduction

    1.   State the general functions of the male and female reproductive systems.

19.2   Organs of the Male Reproductive System

    2.   Name the parts of the male reproductive system, and describe the general functions of each part.

    3.   Outline the process of spermatogenesis.

    4.   Trace the path sperm cells follow from their site of formation to the outside.

19.3   Hormonal Control of Male Reproductive Functions

    5.   Explain how hormones control the activities of the male reproductive organs and the development of male secondary sexual characteristics.

19.4   Organs of the Female Reproductive System

    6.   Name the parts of the female reproductive system, and describe the general functions of each part.

    7.   Outline the process of oogenesis.

19.5   Hormonal Control of Female Reproductive Functions

    8.   Describe how hormones control the activities of female reproductive organs and the development of female secondary sex characteristics.

    9.   Describe the major events that occur during a reproductive cycle.

19.6   Mammary Glands

    10.   Review the structure of the mammary glands.

19.7   Birth Control

    11.   List several methods of birth control, and describe the relative effectiveness of each method.

19.8   Sexually Transmitted Diseases

    12.   List general symptoms of sexually transmitted diseases.

FOCUS QUESTION

How do the male and female reproductive systems assure survival of the species?

MASTERY TEST

Now take the mastery test. Do not guess. As soon as you complete the test, correct it. Note your successes and failures so that you can read the chapter to meet your learning needs.

1. The primary sex organs (gonads) of the male reproductive system are the _____.

2. Male sex cells are produced by the _____ _____ of the seminiferous tubules.

3. The two types of cells in the epithelium of the seminiferous tubules are _____ _____, which support and nourish the _____ _____, which give rise to sperm cells.

4. The enzyme-containing structure that helps the sperm cell penetrate the ovum is the

    a. acrosome.   c. zygote.

    b. flagellum.   d. spermatogonium.

5. Sex cells are produced in a process called _____.

6. How many chromosomes does each spermatogonium contain?

7. During meiosis, the chromosome number is

    a. reduced.   c. unchanged.

    b. increased.

8. The nucleus in the head of the sperm contains _____ chromosomes.

9. The function of the epididymis is to

    a. produce sex hormones.   c. store sperm as they mature.

    b. provide the sperm with mobile tails.   d. supply some of the force needed for ejaculation.

10. Which of the following substances is(are) added to sperm cells by the seminal vesicle?

    a. acid   c. glucose

    b. fructose

11. The function of the secretion of the bulbourethral glands is to

    a. neutralize the acid secretions of the vagina. c. lubricate the penis.

    b. nourish sperm cells.   d. increase the volume of seminal fluid.

12. The process by which sperm cells become capable of fertilizing an ovum is _____.

13. Which of the following is not a male internal accessory organ?

    a. epididymis   c. testes

    b. vas deferens   d. seminal vesicle

14. The external organs of the male reproductive system include the

    a. penis.   c. prostate gland.

    b. testes.   d. scrotum.

15. Exposure to cold causes smooth muscle in the scrotum to (contract/relax).

16. Erection of the penis depends on

    a. contraction of the perineal muscles.   c. enlargement of the glans penis.

    b. filling of the corpus spongiosum with arterial blood.   d. peristaltic contractions of the vas deferens.

17. Emission and ejaculation accompany orgasm.

    a. true   b. false

18. Hormones that control male reproductive functions are secreted from the _____, the _____, and the _____ _____.

19. The pituitary hormone that stimulates the testes to produce testosterone is

    a. gonadotropin-releasing hormone.   c. LH (ICSH).

    b. FSH.   d. ACTH.

0. In the male, growth of body hair, especially in the axilla, face, and pubis, and increased muscle and bone development are examples of _____ _____ characteristics.

1. The hormone that stimulates these changes is _____.

2. The primary sex organs (gonads) of the female reproductive system are the _____.

3. In the ovary, the primary germinal epithelium is located
   a. in the medulla.
   c. in the cortex.
   b. between the medulla and cortex.
   d. on the free surface of the ovary.

24. How many mature egg cells are produced by each primary oocyte?_____

25. At puberty, the primary oocyte matures within the _____ _____.

26. The egg is released from the ovary in a process called _____.

27. Which of the following statements is(are) true about the uterine (fallopian) tubes?
   a. The end of the uterine tube near the ovary has many fingerlike projections called fimbriae.
   c. The inner layer of the ovarian tube is cuboidal epithelium.
   b. The fimbriae are attached to the ovaries.
   d. There are cilia in the lining of the uterine tube that help move the egg toward the uterus.

28. The inner layer of the uterus is the _____.

29. Which of the following statements about the vagina is(are) true?
   a. The mucosal layer contains many mucous glands.
   c. The vagina connects the uterus to the outer surface of the body.
   b. The bulbospongiosus muscle is primarily responsible for closing the vaginal orifice.
   d. The hymen is a membrane that covers the mouth of the cervix.

30. The organ of the female reproductive system that corresponds to the penis is the
   a. vagina.
   c. clitoris.
   b. mons pubis.
   d. labium major.

31. Which of the following tissues become engorged and erect in response to sexual stimulation?
   a. clitoris
   c. outer third of vagina
   b. labia minora
   d. upper third of vagina

32. The hormonal mechanisms that control female reproductive functions are (more, less) complex than in the male.

33. The primary female sex hormones are _____ and _____.

34. Which of the following secondary sex characteristics in the female seem to be related to androgen concentration?
   a. breast development
   c. female skeletal configuration
   b. growth of axillary and pubic hair
   d. deposition of adipose tissue over hips, thighs, buttocks, and breasts

35. During the menstrual cycle, the event that seems to initiate ovulation is
   a. increasing levels of progesterone.
   c. decreasing levels of estrogen.
   b. a sudden increase in concentration of LH.
   d. a cessation of secretion of FSH.

36. After release of the egg, the follicle forms a(n) _____ _____.

37. As the above structure develops, the level of which of the following hormones increases?
   a. estrogen
   c. FSH
   b. progesterone
   d. LH

38. As the hormone levels change in that part of the cycle before and immediately after ovulation, which of the following changes are seen in the uterus?
   a. growth of the myometrium
   c. thickening of the endometrium
   b. increase in adipose cells of the perimetrium
   d. decrease in uterine gland activity

39. The concentration of which of the following hormones decreases following ovulation?
   a. estrogen
   c. FSH
   b. progesterone
   d. LH

40. The cessation of the menstrual cycle in middle age is called _____.

41. Before puberty, the male and female breasts are (similar, dissimilar).

42. The most sensitive test used to detect breast tumors and determine the location of a breast lump is a _____

43. Which of the following contraceptive methods is not a barrier method?

    a.   condoms   c.   contraceptive implants

    b.   spermicides   d.   cervical caps

44. Which of the following contraceptive methods also prevents transmission of sexually transmitted diseases?

    a.   contraceptive pills   c.   condoms

    b.   diaphragm   d.   IUDs

STUDY ACTIVITIES

I. Aids to Understanding Words

Define the following word parts. (pp. 490–491)

andr-   germ-

ejacul-   labi-

fimb-   mens-

follic-   mons-

genesis-   puber-

II. 19.1 Introduction (p. 491)

Describe the functions of the male and female reproductive systems.

III. 19.2 Organs of the Male Reproductive System (pp. 491–499)

A.   1.   Label these structures in the accompanying illustration: urinary bladder, vas deferens, prostate gland, penis, urethra, prepuce, glans penis, epididymis, testis, scrotum, corpus cavernosum, corpus spongiosum, bulbourethral gland, ejaculatory duct, seminal vesicle, symphysis pubis, anus, ureter, large intestine. (p. 498)

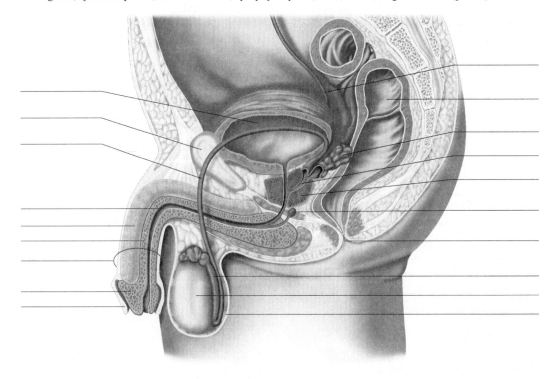

168

2.	What is the primary function of the male reproductive system?

3.	What are the primary organs of the male reproductive system?

B.	Answer these questions concerning the structure of the testes. (pp. 492–493)
	1.	What is the function of spermatogenic cells of the seminiferous tubules?

	2.	What is the function of interstitial cells?

	3.	In what cells does testicular cancer arise?

C.	Describe the process of sperm formation, including where sperm are stored and a description of the sperm. (p. 493)

D.	Answer these questions concerning meiosis. (p. 493)
	1.	What cells undergo meiosis?

	2.	Describe the process of meiosis in sperm.

	3.	What is the result of meiosis in the male?

E.	Answer the following questions about male internal accessory organs. (pp. 494–496)
	1.	List the internal accessory organs of the male reproductive system.

	2.	Answer these questions concerning the epididymis.
		a.	Describe the location and structure of the epididymis.

		b.	What is the function of the epididymis in the emission of sperm?

	3.	Describe the course of the vas deferens.

4. Answer these questions concerning the seminal vesicles.

    a. Where are the seminal vesicles located?

    b. What is the nature and function of the secretion of the seminal vesicles?

5. Answer these questions concerning the prostate gland.

    a. Where is the prostate gland located?

    b. What is the nature and function of the secretion of the prostate gland?

6. Answer these questions concerning the bulbourethral glands.

    a. Describe the location and function of the bulbourethral glands (Cowper's glands).

    b. What is the stimulus for release of this secretion?

7. Describe the seminal fluid.

F. Answer these questions about male external reproductive organs, orgasm, and ejaculation. (pp. 496–498)

    1. What is the structure and function of the scrotum?

    2. Describe the structure of the penis.

    3. Describe the events of erection and ejaculation.

    4. Define male infertility, and list some common causes.

IV. 19.3 Hormonal Control of Male Reproductive Functions (pp. 499–500)

A. Answer these questions concerning pituitary hormones.

    1. What seems to initiate the changes of puberty?

2. What are the functions of FSH and LH?

B. Answer these questions concerning male sex hormones.
   1. Where is testosterone produced?

   2. What is the function of testosterone?

   3. List the male secondary sexual characteristics.

C. Describe the regulation of sex hormones in the male.

V. 19.4 Organs of the Female Reproductive System (pp. 500–506)

A. Label these structures in the accompanying illustration: ovary, uterine tube, uterus, vagina, anus, urinary bladder, urethra, clitoris, labium minor, labium major, symphysis pubis, fimbriae, cervix, rectum, vaginal orifice. (p. 501)

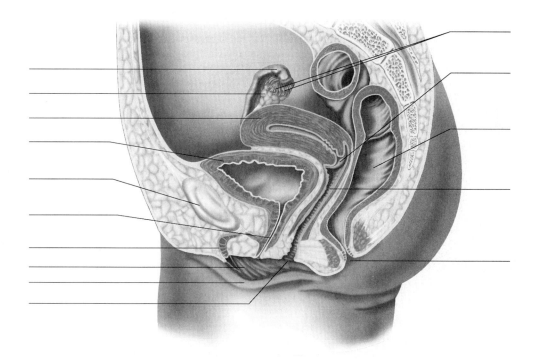

B.   Describe the structure of the ovaries. (pp. 500–501)

C.   Answer these questions concerning the formation of egg cells. (p. 501)
        1.   Outline the process of egg cell production.

        2.   How is this different from spermatogenesis?

D.   Answer these questions concerning the maturation of a follicle. (p. 502)
        1.   What stimulates maturation of a primary follicle at puberty?

        2.   What changes occur in the follicle as a result of maturation?

E.   Answer these questions concerning ovulation. (p. 502)
        1.   What provokes ovulation?

        2.   What happens to the egg after it leaves the ovary?

F.   Answer these questions about female internal accessory organs. (pp. 503–505)
        1.   Label these structures in the accompanying illustration: body of uterus, uterine tube, infundibulum, ovary, cervix, vagina, cervical orifice, fimbriae, follicle, endometrium, myometrium, perimetrium, oocyte.

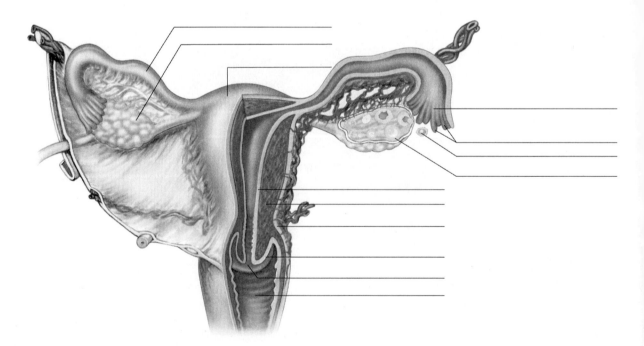

2. How does the structure of the uterine tube move the egg toward the uterus?

3. Answer these questions concerning the uterus.
   a. Based on the description in the text, draw a uterus. Locate the body, cervix, endometrium, myometrium, and perimetrium.

   b. Name the layers of the uterine wall.

4. Answer these questions concerning the vagina.
   a. What is the function of the vagina?

   b. Describe the structure of the vagina.

G. Answer these questions about the female external reproductive organs and erection, lubrication, and orgasm. (pp. 505–506)
    1. To what male organ do the labia majora correspond?

    2. Describe the labia minora.

    3. What is the structure of the clitoris?

    4. Answer these questions concerning the vestibule.
       a. Describe the location of the vestibule.

b. What is the function of the vestibular glands?

5. Describe the events of erection and orgasm in the female.

VI. 19.5 Hormonal Control of Female Reproductive Functions (pp. 506–509)

A. Answer these questions concerning female sex hormones. (pp. 506–507)
   1. What appears to initiate sexual maturation in the female?

   2. What are the sources of female sex hormones?

   3. What is the function of estrogen?

   4. What is the function of progesterone?

   5. What is the function of androgens?

B. Answer these questions concerning female reproductive cycles. (pp. 507–508)
   1. How is a female's first menstrual cycle initiated?

2. Describe the events of the menstrual cycle. Include shifts in hormone levels, uterine changes, and ovarian changes.

3. Why do women athletes experience scant or absent menstrual flow?

C. Answer these questions concerning menopause. (pp. 508–509)
   1. What is menopause?

   2. What seems to be the cause of menopause?

VII. 19.6 Mammary Glands (pp. 509–510)

A. What is the function of the mammary glands? (p. 509)

B. Where are the mammary glands located? (p. 509)

C. Describe the structure of the mammary glands. (pp. 509–510)

D. What is the purpose of monthly breast self-examination? (p. 510)

VIII. 19.7 Birth Control (pp. 510–513)

Describe the various contraceptives in each of the categories listed.

Coitus interruptus

Rhythm method

Mechanical barriers

Chemical barriers

Combined Hormone Contraceptives

Injectable contraceptives

Intrauterine devices

Surgical methods

IX. 19.8 Sexually Transmitted Diseases (pp. 513–514)

A.   List the symptoms of sexually transmitted diseases.

B.   What are the male and female complications of STDs?

X. Clinical Focus Question

Compare the various methods of contraception. How do moral and ethical factors influence an individual's contraceptive choices?

When you have finished the study activities to your satisfaction, retake the mastery test and compare your results with your initial attempt. If you are not satisfied with your performance, repeat the appropriate study activities.

CHAPTER **20**

PREGNANCY, GROWTH, AND DEVELOPMENT

OVERVIEW

This chapter describes the events of fertilization and the changes that take place in the maternal body during pregnancy and childbirth (objectives 2, 3, 4, 5, 6, 7, 11, and 12). It also covers the events of embryonic and fetal development, and the adjustments of the infant to extrauterine life (objectives 8, 9, 10, and 13). The concepts of growth and development are also covered (objective 1). Genetics, the science of inheritance, is also discussed (objectives 14, 15).

CHAPTER OBJECTIVES

After you have studied this chapter, you should be able to:

20.1   Introduction
1. Distinguish between growth and development.
2. Distinguish between the prenatal and postnatal periods.

20.2   Pregnancy
3. Define *pregnancy,* and describe the process of fertilization.

20.3   Prenatal Period
4. Describe the major events of cleavage.
5. Distinguish between an embryo and a fetus.
6. Describe the formation and function of the placenta.
7. Describe the hormonal changes in the maternal body during pregnancy.
8. Explain how the primary germ layers originate, and list the structures each layer produces.
9. Describe the major events of the embryonic stage of development.
10. Describe the major events of the fetal stage of development.
11. Trace the general path of blood through the fetal circulatory system.
12. Describe the birth process, and explain the role of hormones in this process.

20.4   Postnatal Period
13. Describe the major cardiovascular and physiological adjustments required of the newborn.

20.5   Genetics
14. Distinguish among the modes of inheritance.
15. Describe the occurrence of multifactorial traits.

FOCUS QUESTION

How is a unique individual produced from the union of two cells?

MASTERY TEST

Now take the mastery test. Do not guess. As soon as you complete the test, correct it. Note your successes and failures so that you can read the chapter to meet your learning needs.

1.   An increase in size and number of cells is referred to as _____.
2.   Fertilization takes place in the
    a.   vagina.
    b.   cervix.
    c.   uterus.
    d.   uterine tube.

3. Which of the following is thought to be the mechanism by which the sperm enters the egg?

a. An antigen-antibody reaction briefly alters the cell membrane of the egg.

b. The structure of the cell membrane of the egg allows entry.

c. The head of the sperm has an enzyme that permits digestion through the membrane of the egg.

d. The mechanism is unknown.

4. Female infertility can be due to

a. hypersecretion of pituitary gonadotropic hormones.

b. endometriosis.

c. scarring of the uterine tubes.

d. mucus plug in the cervix secondary to infection.

5. The first phase in embryonic development is called _____.

6. Implantation takes place by the end of _____ week(s) following fertilization.

7. The hormone that maintains the corpus luteum following implantation is

a. LH.

b. HCG.

c. progesterone.

d. FSH.

8. The primary source of hormones needed to support a pregnancy after the first three months is the

_____.

9. Breast development during pregnancy is stimulated by _____ _____.

10. The ectoderm, mesoderm, and endoderm are _____ _____ layers.

11. From which of the layers of the embryonic disk do the hair, nails, and glands of the skin arise?

a. endoderm

b. ectoderm

c. mesoderm

12. Which of the following structures arises from the mesoderm?

a. lining of the mouth

b. muscle

c. lining of the respiratory tract

d. epidermis

13. At what time does the embryonic disk become a cylinder?

a. four weeks of development

b. six weeks of development

c. eight weeks of development

d. four days of development

14. The chorion in contact with the endometrium becomes the _____.

15. The membrane covering the embryo is called the _____.

16. The vessels in the umbilical cord are

a. one artery and one vein.

b. one artery and two veins.

c. two arteries and one vein.

d. two arteries and two veins.

17. In the embryo, blood cells are formed in the

a. amnion.

b. placenta.

c. allantois.

d. yolk sac.

18. A factor that damages the embryo during a period of rapid growth is a _____.

19. The embryonic stage ends at _____ weeks.

20. Pregnancy can be diagnosed ten days after fertilization by testing the urine of the woman for which of the following substances?

a. estrogen

b. progesterone

c. human chorionic gonadotropin

d. amniotic fluid

21. At the beginning of the fetal stage of development, (most, few) of the body structures are formed.

22. Skeletal muscles become active in the _____ lunar month.

23. A fetus is full term at the end of the _____ lunar month.

24. Oxygen and nutrient-rich blood reach the fetus from the placenta via the umbilical _____.

5.   The ductus venosus shunts blood around the

    a.   liver.   c.   pancreas.

    b.   spleen.   d.   small intestine.

6.   The structures that allow blood to avoid the nonfunctioning fetal lungs are the _____
_____ and the _____ _____.

27.   Labor is initiated by a decrease in _____ levels and secretion of _____
by the posterior pituitary gland.

28.   Bleeding following expulsion of the afterbirth is controlled by

    a.   hormonal mechanisms.   c.   contraction of the uterine muscles.

    b.   increased fibrinogen levels.   d.   sympathetic stimulation of arterioles.

29.   Milk production is stimulated by the hormone _____.

30.   Milk is secreted from the breast

    a.   as production fills the duct structure.   c.   in response to mechanical stimulation of the nipple (i.e., sucking).

    b.   in response to hormonal stimulation.   d.   in response to gonadotropins.

31.   The factor that decreases the effort required for an infant to breathe after the first breath is _____.

32.   The primary energy source for the newborn is

    a.   glucose.   c.   protein.

    b.   fat.

33.   An infant's urine is (more, less) concentrated than an adult's.

34.   Which of the following fetal structures closes as a result of a change in pressure?

    a.   ductus venosus   c.   umbilical vessels

    b.   ductus arteriosus   d.   foramen ovale

35.   The science that studies why individuals vary in terms of a variety of characteristics is _____.

STUDY ACTIVITIES

I.   Aids to Understanding Words

Define the following word parts. (p. 521)

allant-   morul-

chorio-   nat-

cleav-   troph-

lacun-   umbil-

II.   20.1 Introduction (p. 521)

Define *growth* and *development*. (p. 521)

III.   20.2 Pregnancy (pp. 521–522)

A.   Define pregnancy.

B.   How is the oocyte fertilized?

IV.   **20.3 Prenatal Period (pp. 523–538)**

A.   Describe the events of pregnancy from fertilization to implantation. (pp. 522–523)

B.   Describe the hormonal changes that occur in the mother during pregnancy. (pp. 525–526)

C.   Define and list common causes of female infertility. (p. 525)

D.   Answer these questions concerning the embryonic stage. (pp. 526–530)
          1.   What are the boundaries that define the embryonic stage of development?

          2.   What is the embryonic disk?

          3.   What are the primary germ layers?

          4.   List the structures that arise from these primary germ layers.
                ectoderm

                mesoderm

                endoderm

          5.   Describe the structure and function of the umbilical cord and fetal membranes.

          6.   What is the function of the allantois and the yolk sac?

7. How do teratogens affect the developing fetus?

E. Fill in the following table. (pp. 530–538)

The fetal stage

Month	Major events of growth and development
Third lunar month	
Fourth lunar month	
Fifth lunar month	
Sixth lunar month	
Seventh lunar month	
Eighth lunar month	
Ninth lunar month	

F. Describe the following prenatal tests. (pp. 536–537)
    1. chorionic villus sampling

    2. amniocentesis

3.   fetal cell sorting

G.   Trace a drop of fetal blood from the placenta through the circulatory system of the fetus. Identify the difference from postnatal circulation. (pp. 532–534)

H.   Answer these questions concerning the birth process. (pp. 534–538)

   1.   What changes take place in placental hormone secretion after the seventh month of gestation?

   2.   What stimulates secretion of oxytocin?

   3.   What regulates secretion of oxytocin?

   4.   What is labor?

   5.   What is afterbirth?

   6.   How is bleeding controlled once the uterus is emptied?

V.   **20.4 Postnatal Period (pp. 538–540)**

A.   Describe the production and secretion of milk. (pp. 538–539)

B.   Fill in the following table. (pp. 539–540)

The neonatal period

Life function	Major changes needed to adjust to extrauterine life
Respiration	
Nutrition	
Urine formation	
Temperature control	
Circulation	

VI.   Genetics (pp. 540–544)

      A.   1.   Inherited traits are determined by DNA sequences called _____.
              2.   The study of how specific characteristics are inherited is known as _____.
              3.   The environment can influence the way genes are expressed. (true/false) _____
      B.   Patterns of inheritance seen in different generations of a family are called _____
             _____.
      C.   1.   A way of displaying the 23 chromosome pairs is called a
                   a. genetic map   c. genetic code
                   b. karyotype   d. phenotype
              2.   The X and Y chromosomes determine _____.
              3.   Chromosome pairs 1 through 23 are _____.
              4.   Variant forms of a gene are called _____.
              5.   The combination of alleles for a gene constitutes an individual's _____. The appearance of a health condition associated with a particular combination of alleles is the individual's _____.

VII.   Clinical Focus Question

What advice would you give to a young woman who is considering becoming pregnant? How would the woman's age, education, family history, and economic status influence your answer?

When you have finished the study activities to your satisfaction, retake the mastery test and compare your results with your initial attempt. If you are not satisfied with your performance, repeat the appropriate study activities.

MASTERY TEST ANSWERS

1 Mastery Test Answers

1. c
2. b
3. c
4. Latin and Greek
5. anatomy
6. physiology
7. always
8. b
9. movement, responsiveness, growth, reproduction, respiration, digestion, absorption, circulation, assimilation, excretion
10. yes
11. water
12. energy, living matter
13. energy
14. increases
15. hydrostatic
16. a
17. 1. d; 2. b; 3. c
18. atoms, molecules, cell, tissue, organ, organ system
19. axial portion
20. appendicular
21. dorsal, ventral
22. diaphragm
23. mediastinum
24. a, b, c
25. oral, nasal, orbital, middle ear
26. pleural cavity
27. pericardial
28. abdominopelvic
29. integumentary
30. a-3, b-4, c-2, d-2, e-4, f-2, g-2, h-3, i-2, j-1
31. b, c
32. c
33. b
34. body regions

2 Mastery Test Answers

1. a
2. chemistry
3. Matter is anything that has weight and takes up space. It occurs in the forms of solids, liquids, and gases.
4. elements
5. carbon, hydrogen, oxygen, and nitrogen
6. e
7. a-3, b-1, c-2
8. protons
9. a
10. c
11. the outer shell of its atoms has its maximum number of electrons
12. protons and neutrons
13. a
14. a
15. a
16. polar
17. different
18. molecular
19. structural
20. synthesis, decomposition
21. reversible
22. catalyst
23. acid
24. bases
25. hydrogen ions
26. 7
27. electrolyte
28. a. I, b. O, c. O, d. I, e. O, f. O
29. carbon, hydrogen, oxygen
30. fatty acids, glycerol
31. lipids
32. protein
33. denatured
34. a

3 Mastery Test Answers

1. shape
2. b
3. a, b
4. cytoplasm, nucleus
5. b
6. selectively permeable
7. c
8. b
9. water
10. membrane-spanning, trans-membrane
11. sodium, potassium
12. endoplasmic reticulum
13. a
14. outside
15. energy
16. b
17. Liver, kidneys
18. movement
19. d
20. b
21. nucleolus, chromatin
22. cellular energy
23. diffusion
24. facilitated diffusion
25. osmosis
26. a
27. filtration
28. active transport
29. pinocytosis
30. phagocytosis
31. b
32. mitosis
33. a-2, b-4, c-1, d-3
34. differentiation

4 Mastery Test Answers

1. c
2. anabolic metabolism
3. catabolic metabolism
4. a
5. c
6. protein
7. hydrolysis
8. c
9. enzyme
10. b

11. b
12. enzyme, substrate, efficiency
13. coenzyme
14. a
15. oxidation
16. anaerobic respiration
17. aerobic respiration
18. oxygen
19. ATP molecules
20. metabolic pathway
21. a, c
22. DNA (deoxyribonucleic acid)
23. adenine, thymine, cytosine, guanine
24. nucleus, cytoplasm
25. messenger, transfer
26. uracil
27. c
28. mutation
29. rate-limiting enzyme
30. d
31. Interphase

5 Mastery Test Answers

1. epithelial, connective, muscle, and nervous tissue
2. similar
3. b
4. a, c, d
5. a-4, b-1, c-5, d-2, e-3
6. transitional epithelium
7. exocrine
8. serous
9. a, b, d
10. fixed
11. c
12. collagen
13. elastin
14. b
15. a, b, c, d
16. hyaline
17. fibrocartilage
18. slowly
19. bone
20. plasma
21. smooth, skeletal, cardiac
22. nervous
23. organ

24. serous, mucous, cutaneous, synovial
25. b
26. c

6 Mastery Test Answers

1. epidermis
2. dermis
3. subcutaneous layer
4. b
5. a
6. equal
7. dermis
8. heat insulator
9. arrector pili muscles
10. c
11. keratinization
12. a, c
13. sweat
14. melanoma
15. b
16. c
17. a
18. deep

7 Mastery Test Answers

1. b
2. b
3. d
4. compact
5. spongy or cancellous
6. marrow
7. intramembranous bones
8. endochondral bones
9. d
10. osteocytes; osteoclasts
11. is remodeled
12. a, c
13. cartilaginous callus
14. levers
15. a, c
16. c
17. b, d
18. b
19. skull, hyoid, vertebral column, thoracic cage

20. pectoral girdle, arms or upper limbs, pelvic girdle, legs or lower limbs
21. c
22. b
23. occipital
24. maxillary
25. fontanels
26. b
27. c
28. a, b, c, d
29. thoracic vertebrae, sternum
30. clavicles, scapulae
31. radius
32. a
33. a
34. c
35. b
36. c
37. b
38. a
39. b

8 Mastery Test Answers

1. a
2. skeletal muscle tissue, blood, nervous tissue, connective tissue
3. fascia
4. b
5. actin, myosin
6. mild muscle strain
7. c
8. motor unit
9. a
10. acetylcholine
11. adenosine triphosphate or ATP
12. creatine phosphate
13. b
14. a, c, d
15. lactic acid
16. threshold stimulus
17. c
18. a
19. a
20. decrease
21. multiunit, visceral
22. a, c

23. more slowly
24. rapidly
25. origin, insertion
26. antagonists
27. d
28. a
29. b
30. linea alba
31. b

9 Mastery Test Answers

1. neuron
2. d
3. a
4. b
5. c
6. sensory, integrative, motor
7. somatic
8. neuroglial
9. c
10. yes
11. c
12. axonal hillock
13. bipolar, unipolar, multipolar
14. sensory, interneuron, motor
15. sodium
16. permeability
17. larger, smaller
18. synapse
19. neurotransmitters
20. processing
21. a, c
22. nerve
23. reflex
24. a
25. c
26. c
27. b, d
28. cerebrum, brain stem, cerebellum
29. a
30. a-3, b-4, c-3, d-1, e-2, f-1
31. left
32. choroid plexuses
33. d
34. b
35. limbic system

36. reticular formation
37. cerebellum
38. somatic, autonomic
39. 12, brain stem
40. 2-6
41. 31
42. autonomic
43. thorax, sacrum
44. a, b
45. c, d

10 Mastery Test Answers

1. chemoreceptors—change in concentration of chemicals; pain receptors—tissue damage; thermoreceptors—change in temperature; mechanoreceptors—change in pressure or movement; photoreceptors—light energy
2. c
3. skin, muscles, joints, viscera
4. a
5. c
6. chemicals
7. a, c
8. acute
9. reticular formation
10. endorphins
11. smell, taste, hearing, equilibrium (static, dynamic), sight
12. b
13. c
14. olfactory nerve or tracts
15. c
16. b
17. sweet, salty, sour, bitter
18. equilibrium
19. c, d
20. eustachian tube (auditory tube)
21. osseous labyrinth, membranous labyrinth
22. a
23. a
24. semicircular canals
25. c
26. cornea
27. a

28. b
29. optic nerve
30. a
31. cornea
32. pupil
33. retina
34. b
35. refraction
36. rods, cones
37. a-1, b-2, c-1, d-2
38. rhodopsin, opsin, retinal
39. optic chiasma

11 Mastery Test Answers

1. phenomes
2. hormone
3. paracrine, autocrine
4. exocrine
5. endocrine
6. a
7. b
8. prostaglandins
9. a, b
10. hypothalamus
11. hypothalamus
12. a, b
13. a, b, c
14. prolactin
15. a, d
16. b
17. a
18. thyroxine, triiodothyronine
19. c, d
20. iodine
21. calcitonin
22. b, d
23. a, b, c
24. a, d
25. epinephrine, norepinephrine
26. a
27. a, b, c
28. male
29. islets of Langerhans
30. glucagon
31. b, d
32. type II
33. b

4. infection
5. a
6. a

2 Mastery Test Answers

1. connective
2. 55
3. b
4. a, b, d
5. erythropoietin
6. 120 days
7. b
8. yes
9. a
10. b
11. interleukins; colony-stimulating factors
12. a
13. b
14. 5,000, 10,000
15. a, c
16. histamine, heparin
17. platelet or thrombocyte
18. a-3, b-1, c-2, d-2, e-3
19. c
20. b, d
21. b
22. fibrinogen, fibrin
23. a, c
24. d
25. positive feedback
26. embolus
27. b
28. a
29. c

13 Mastery Test Answers

1. mediastinum
2. a
3. a
4. no
5. c
6. atria, ventricles
7. a, d
8. b
9. a
10. coronary arteries
11. b

12. cardiac cycle
13. b
14. b
15. a
16. electrocardiogram
17. a
18. decrease
19. b, c
20. vasoconstriction
21. plaque, atherosclerosis
22. c
23. b, d
24. filtration, osmosis, diffusion
25. a
26. a
27. b
28. valves
29. b
30. stroke volume
31. heart action, blood volume, viscosity, peripheral resistance
32. c
33. parasympathetic
34. b
35. a
36. d
37. left atrium
38. brachiocephalic artery, common carotid artery, left subclavian artery
39. common iliac

14 Mastery Test Answers

1. lymphatic
2. lymphatic capillaries, collecting ducts
3. b
4. b
5. c
6. a, c
7. veins
8. edema
9. c
10. d
11. b
12. thymosin, T cells
13. spleen
14. b, d

15. pathogens
16. c
17. a, d
18. redness, swelling, heat, pain
19. c
20. adaptive immunity
21. thymus gland
22. antigens
23. d
24. cell-mediated immunity
25. d
26. G, A, M
27. complement
28. accessory cell
29. d
30. passive
31. b
32. lymphocytes, helper T cells
33. tissue rejection reaction

15 Mastery Test Answers

1. a
2. alimentary canal
3. accessory organs
4. a
5. d
6. mixing, propelling
7. no
8. frenulum
9. c
10. c
11. a
12. a, b
13. d
14. increase
15. b
16. peristalsis
17. b
18. c
19. b
20. vitamin B_{12}
21. a
22. b
23. inhibits
24. chyme
25. a
26. a

27. a
28. b, c, d
29. alkaline
30. upper right
31. d
32. a
33. d
34. Kuppfer
35. bile salts
36. a, d
37. cholecystokinin
38. a, b, d
39. duodenum, jejunum, ileum
40. b
41. most
42. are
43. diarrhea
44. cecum
45. b
46. electrolytes, water
47. a, c
48. water
49. essential nutrients
50. a, b
51. cellulose
52. b, d
53. d
54. linoleic acid
55. cholesterol
56. a, c, d
57. amino acids
58. complete
59. calcium, phosphorus
60. oxygen

16 Mastery Test Answers

1. respiration
2. a-1, b-2, c-2, d-1, e-3
3. nasal cavity, larynx
4. b, c
5. a
6. c
7. alveolar ducts
8. visceral pleura
9. parietal pleura
10. emphysema
11. larger
12. b
13. contracts, increasing, decreasing
14. c
15. pleural
16. surfactant
17. b, c
18. d
19. brain stem
20. a
21. carbon dioxide
22. alveolus, capillary
23. pressure
24. partial pressure
25. hemoglobin
26. c

17 Mastery Test Answers

1. b, d
2. b, c
3. a, b, c
4. renal pelvis
5. d
6. d
7. a, b
8. a
9. efferent arteriole
10. Juxtaglomerular
11. urine
12. b
13. hydrostatic pressure
14. c
15. d
16. renin, blood pressure
17. d
18. a
19. b
20. d
21. b, d
22. d
23. ureters
24. c
25. cystitis

26. trigone
27. b
28. urgency
29. b
30. a

18 Mastery Test Answers

1. equal
2. c
3. intracellular
4. extracellular
5. d
6. hydrostatic
7. osmotic
8. a
9. c
10. c
11. d
12. food, beverages
13. perspiration, feces, urine
14. aldosterone
15. parathyroid hormone
16. hydrogen ion
17. b
18. c
19. combine with
20. c
21. c
22. rate, depth
23. c
24. respiratory
25. a, c, d

19 Mastery Test Answers

1. testes
2. spermatogenic cells
3. supporting cells, spermatogenic cells
4. a
5. meiosis
6. 46
7. a
8. 23
9. c
10. b
11. c
12. capacitation
13. c

4. a, d
5. contract
6. b
7. a
8. testes, hypothalamus, anterior pituitary gland
9. c
20. secondary sexual
21. testosterone
22. ovaries
23. d
24. 1
25. primary follicle
26. ovulation
27. a, d
28. endometrium
29. b, c
30. c
31. a, c
32. more
33. estrogen, progesterone
34. b, c
35. b
36. corpus luteum
37. b
38. c
39. c, d

40. menopause
41. similar
42. mammography
43. c
44. c

20 Mastery Test Answers

1. growth
2. d
3. c
4. a, b, c, d
5. cleavage
6. one
7. b
8. placenta
9. placental lactogen
10. primary germ
11. b
12. b
13. a
14. placenta
15. amnion
16. c
17. c, d

18. teratogen
19. 8
20. c
21. most
22. 5th
23. 10th
24. vein
25. a
26. foramen ovale, ductus arteriosus
27. progesterone, oxytocin
28. c
29. prolactin
30. c
31. surfactant
32. b
33. less
34. d
35. genetics

Notes

Notes

Notes

Notes

Notes

Notes

Notes

Notes

Notes

Notes

Notes

Notes